PARTY SONGS

T0066105

ISBN-13: 978-1-4234-2132-0
ISBN-10: 1-4234-2132-9

HAL•LEONARD®
CORPORATION
7777 W. BLUEMOUND RD. P.O. BOX 13819 MILWAUKEE, WI 53213

Visit Hal Leonard Online at
www.halleonard.com

THE CHICKEN DANCE

By TERRY RENDALL
and WERNER THOMAS

1. Do you wan-na feel good,
2.-4. *(See additional lyrics)*

wan-na laugh and play? (Let's laugh and play.) Wan-na have some fun,

throw your blues a - way? (Your blues a - way.) Are you feel - in' sad?

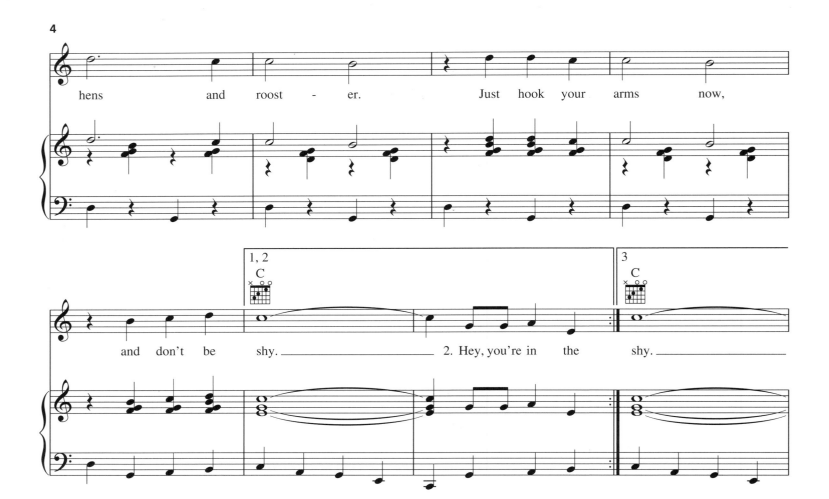

hens and roost - er. Just hook your arms now,

1, 2 C and don't be shy. _____ 2. Hey, you're in the **3** C shy. _____

D.S. al Coda
_____ 4. Now we're al - most

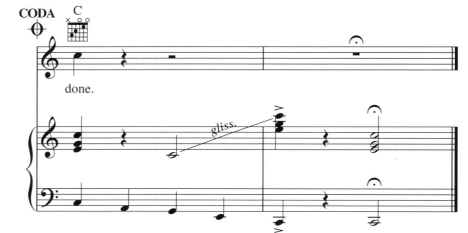

CODA C
done.

gliss.

Additional Lyrics

2. Hey, you're in the swing.
   You're cluckin' like a bird. (Pluck, pluck, pluck, pluck.)
   You're flappin' your wings.
   Don't you feel absurd. (No, no, no, no.)
   It's a chicken dance,
   Like a rooster and a hen. (Ya, ya, ya, ya.)
   Flappy chicken dance;
   Let's do it again. *(To Chorus 2:)*

Chorus 2:
   Relax and let the music move you.
   Let all your inhibitions go.
   Just watch your partner whirl around you.
   We're havin' fun now; I told you so.

3. Now you're flappin' like a bird
   And you're wigglin' too. (I like that move.)
   You're without a care.
   It's a dance for you. (Just made for you.)
   Keep doin' what you do.
   Don't you cop out now. (Don't cop out now.)
   Gets better as you dance;
   Catch your breath somehow. *(To Chorus 3:)*

4. Now we're almost through,
   Really flyin' high. (Bye, bye, bye, bye.)
   All you chickens and birds,
   Time to say goodbye. (To say goodbye.)
   Goin' back to the nest,
   But the flyin' was fun. (Oh, it was fun.)
   Chicken dance was the best,
   But the dance is done.

COPACABANA
(At the Copa)

Music by BARRY MANILOW
Lyric by BRUCE SUSSMAN and JACK FELDMAN

Moderately, with a Latin feel

Her name was Lo - la; ___ she was a
Ri - co; ___ he wore a
Lo - la; ___ she was a

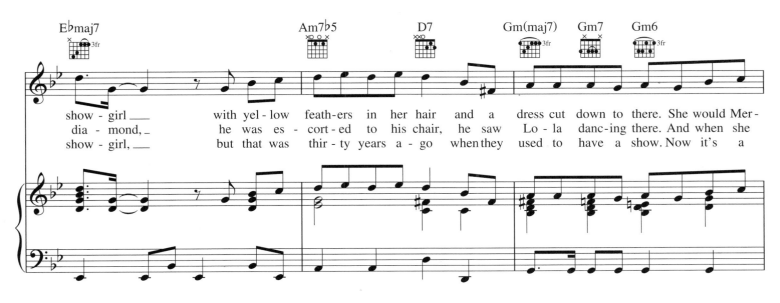

show - girl ___ with yel - low feath - ers in her hair and a dress cut down to there. She would Mer-
dia - mond, ___ he was es - cort - ed to his chair, he saw Lo - la danc - ing there. And when she
show - girl, ___ but that was thir - ty years a - go when they used to have a show. Now it's a

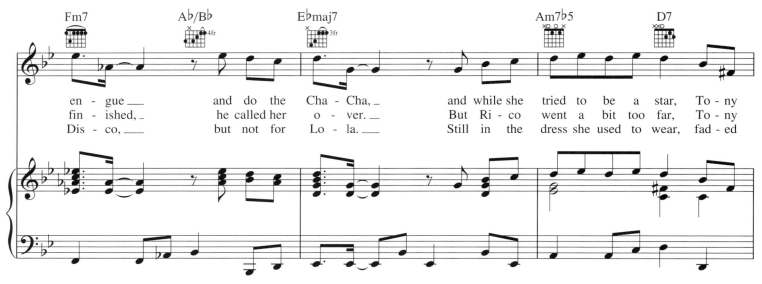

en - gue ___ and do the Cha - Cha, ___ and while she tried to be a star, To - ny
fin - ished, ___ he called her o - ver. ___ But Ri - co went a bit too far, To - ny
Dis - co, ___ but not for Lo - la. Still in the dress she used to wear, fad - ed

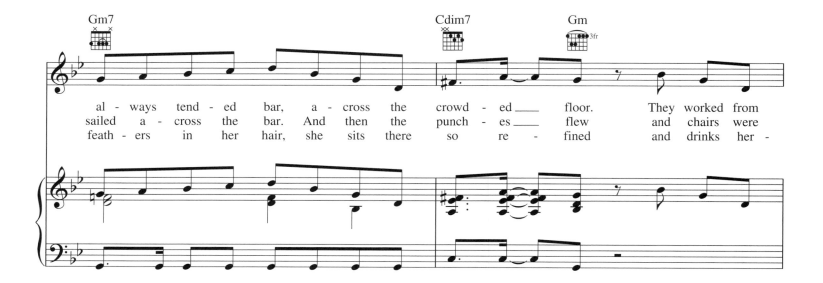

al - ways tend - ed bar, a - cross the crowd - ed ___ floor. They worked from
sailed a - cross the bar. And then the punch - es ___ flew and chairs were
feath - ers in her hair, she sits there so re - fined and drinks her-

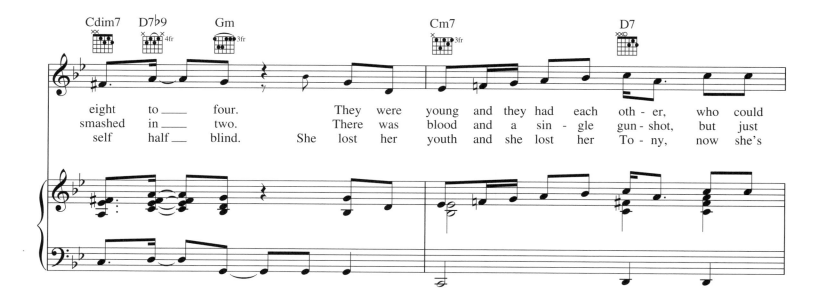

eight to ___ four. They were young and they had each oth - er, who could
smashed in ___ two. There was blood and a sin - gle gun - shot, but just
self half ___ blind. She lost her youth and she lost her To - ny, now she's

ask for more? }
who shot who? } At the Co - pa, ___ Co - pa - ca - ban - a, ___ the
lost her mind. }

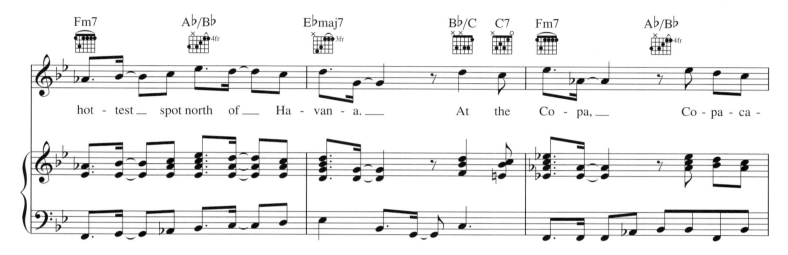

hot - test ___ spot north of ___ Ha - van - a. ___ At the Co - pa, ___ Co - pa - ca -

ban - a, ___ mu - sic ___ and pas - sion ___ were al - ways ___ the fash - ion, at the

To Coda ⊕

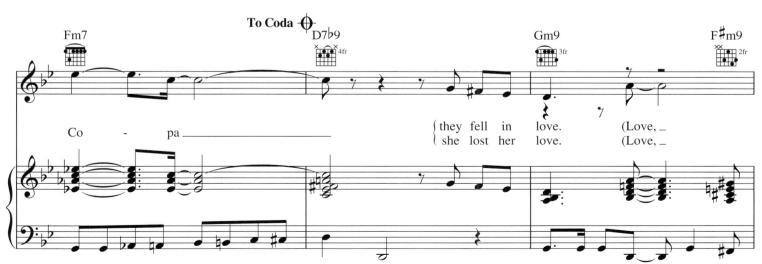

Co - pa _____

{ they fell in love. (Love, ___
{ she lost her love. (Love, ___

Co - pa - ca - ban - a.) __
Co - pa - ca - ban - a.) __
His name was

Co - pa, _____ Co - pa - ca -

ban - a, _____ Co - pa - ca - ban - a, _____

ah, _____

Ah,_____ Ah,_____

_____ Ah._____

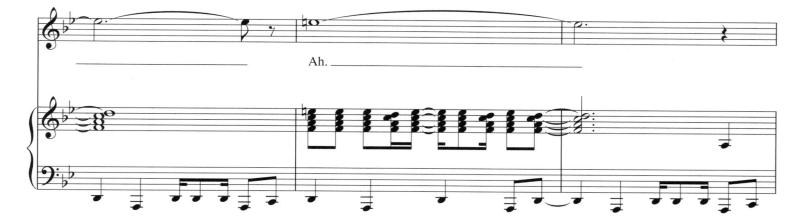

Ah._____

Co - pa,_____ Co - pa - ca -

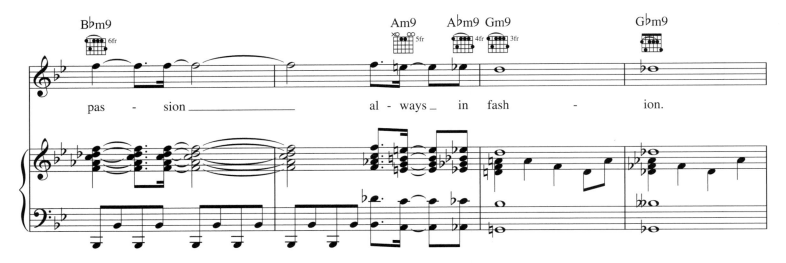

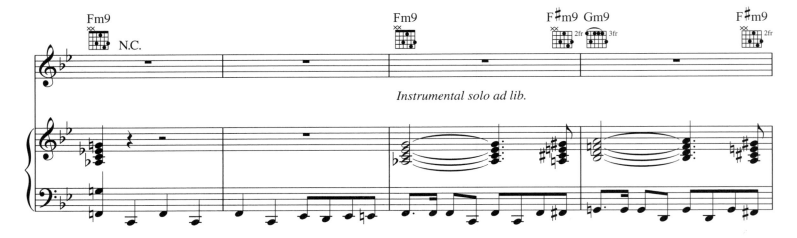

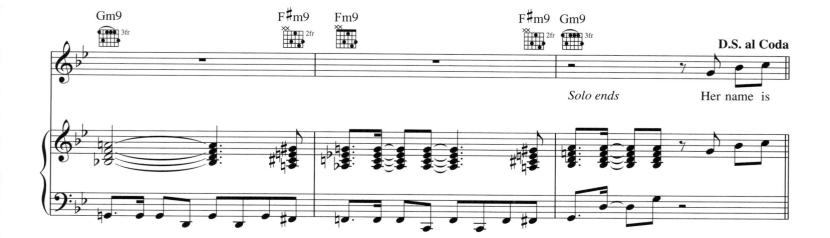

DANCING QUEEN

Words and Music by BENNY ANDERSSON,
BJÖRN ULVAEUS and STIG ANDERSON

Strong Rock

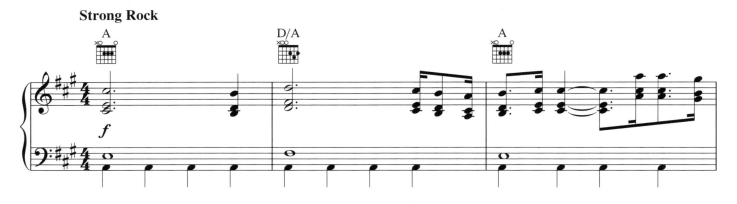

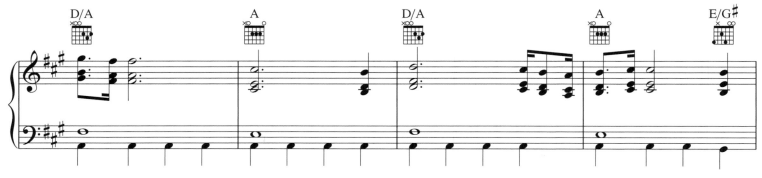

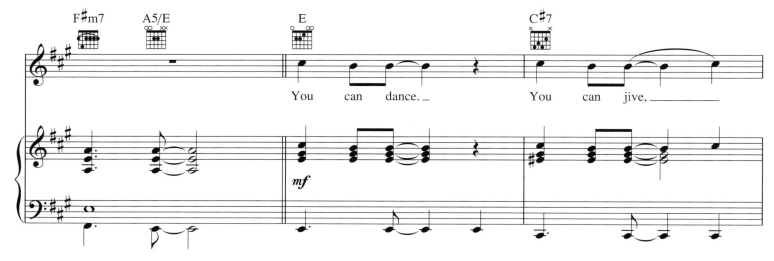

You can dance.___ You can jive,_____

hav-ing___ the time of___ your life.____ Oh,_____ see that___ girl.____

Watch that __ scene, __ dig-gin' the danc-ing __ queen. __

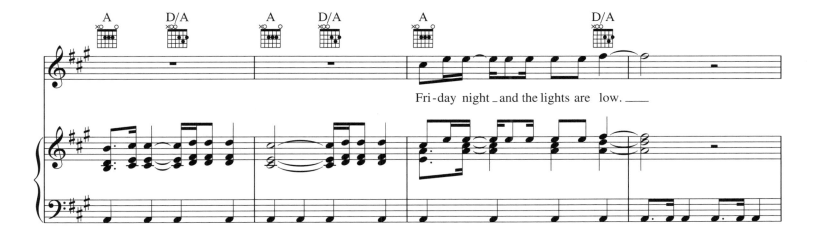

Fri-day night __ and the lights are low. __

Look-ing out __ for a place to go, _____ oh, _____ where they play __ the right mu - sic.

Get-ting in ___ the swing, _ you come to look for a king. _

An-y-bod-y could be that guy.___
You're a teas-er. You turn 'em on,___

Night is young___ and the mu-sic's
leave 'em burn-ing and then you're

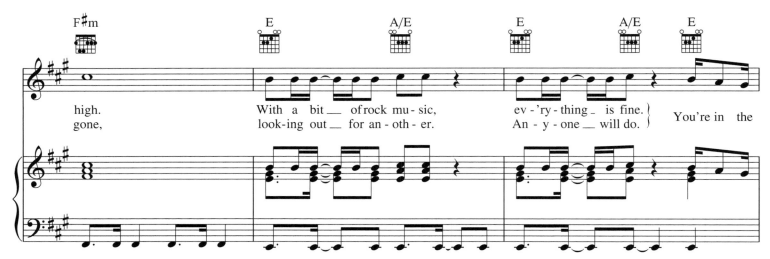

high.
gone,

With a bit___ of rock mu-sic,
look-ing out___ for an-oth-er.

ev-'ry-thing___ is fine.
An-y-one___ will do.

You're in the

mood for a dance,___ and when___ you get the___ chance,_____

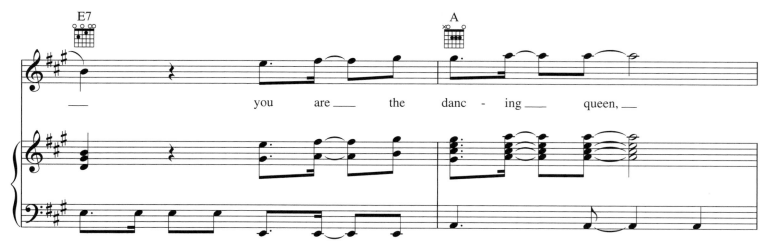

___ you are ___ the danc-ing ___ queen, ___

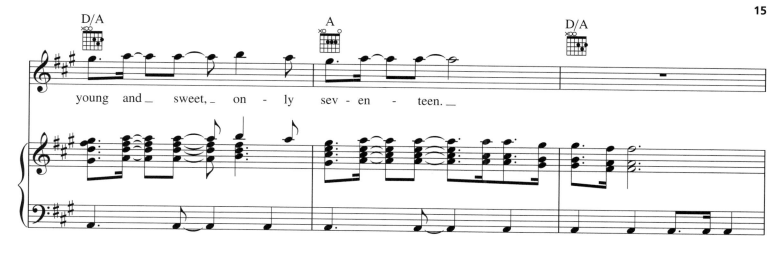

young and_ sweet,_ on - ly sev - en - teen._

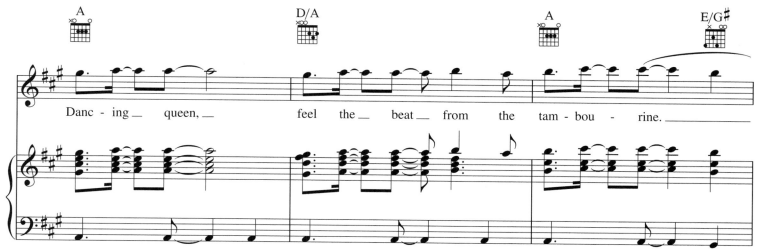

Danc - ing_ queen,_ feel the_ beat from the tam - bou - rine. _____

_____ You can dance._ You can jive, _____

hav - ing_ the time of_ your life. _____ Oh, _____ see that_ girl. _

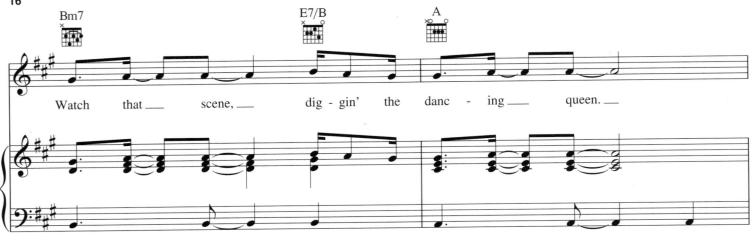

Watch that ___ scene, ___ dig - gin' the danc - ing ___ queen. ___

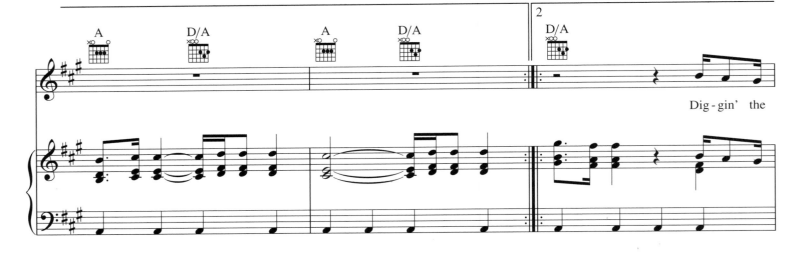

Dig - gin' the

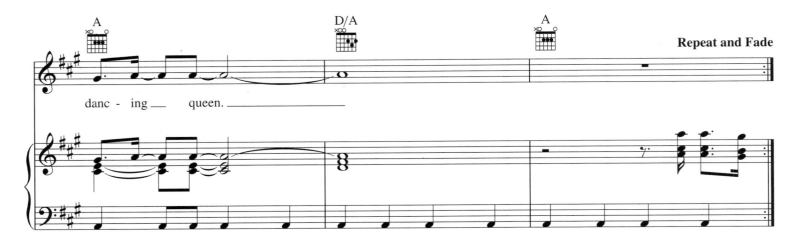

danc - ing ___ queen. ___

Repeat and Fade

HOT HOT HOT

Words and Music by
ALPHONSUS CASSELL

Moderate Latin Dance

O - lé, o - lé, o - lé, o - lé. O - lé, o - lé, o -

lé, o - lé.

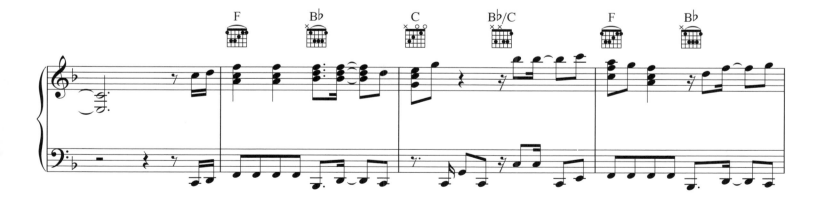

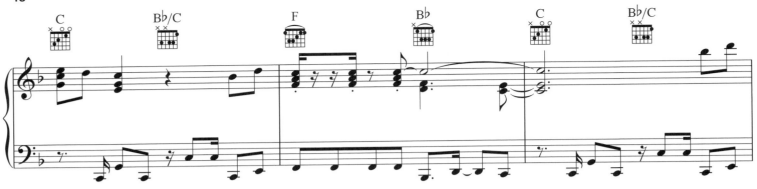

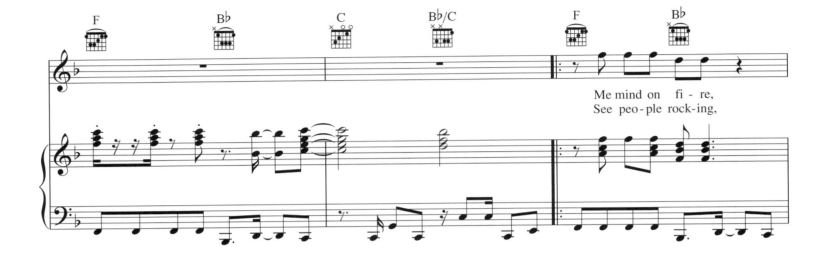

Me mind on fi - re,
See peo - ple rock-ing,

me soul on fi - re, feel-ing hot, hot, __ hot!
hear peo-ple chant-ing, feel-ing hot, hot, __ hot!

All the peo - ple, all a - round me, feel - ing
Keep up the spir - it, come on let's hear it, feel - ing

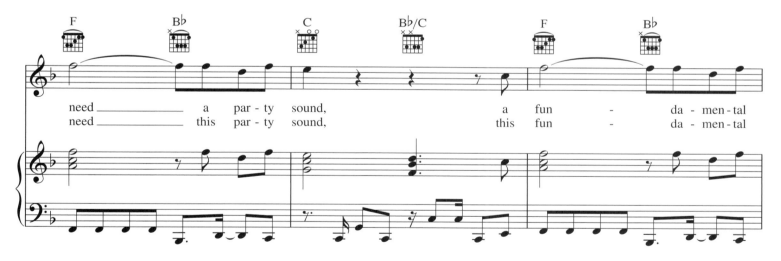

20

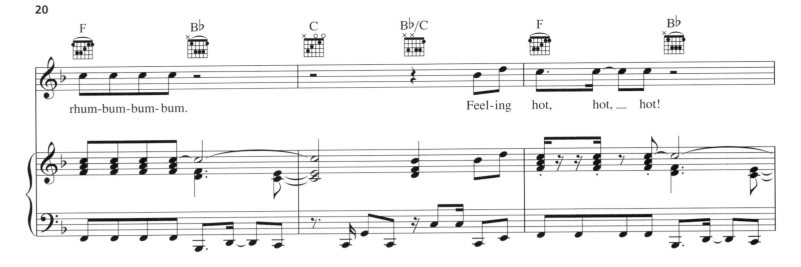

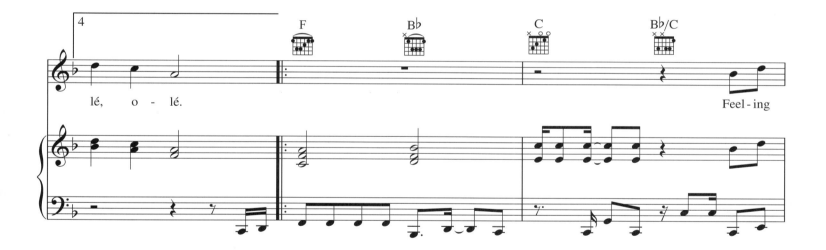

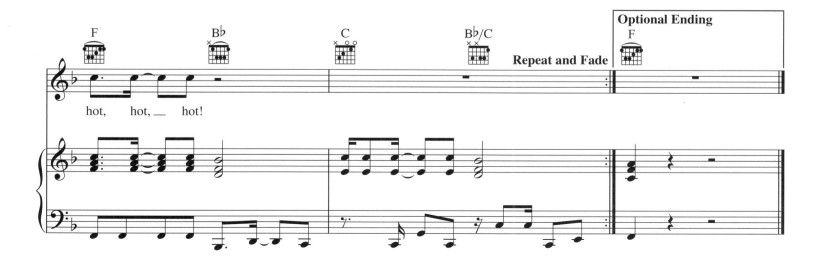

ELECTRIC SLIDE

Words and Music by
NEVILLE LIVINGSTON

(1., 3.) You can't see ____ it. }
(2.) Some say it's a mys - tic. }
(It's e -

lec - tric.)
{ You've got to feel ____ it. }
{ You can't re - sist ____ it. }
(It's e -

lec - tric.)
{ Ooh, ____ it's shock - ing. }
{ You can't do with - out it. }
(It's e -

*Recorded a half step lower.

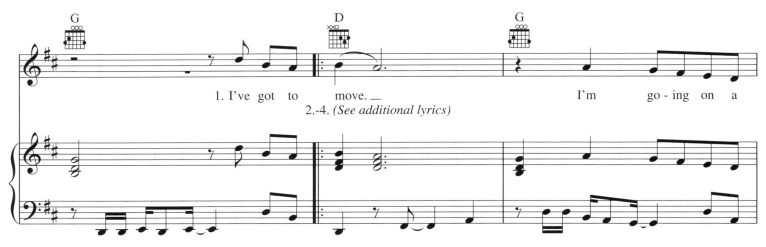

1. I've got to move. ___
2.-4. *(See additional lyrics)*

I'm go-ing on a

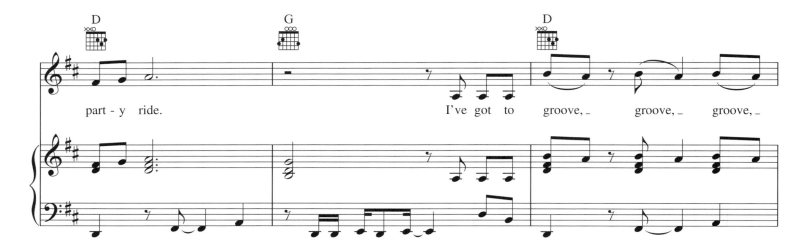

part-y ride.

I've got to groove, ___ groove, ___ groove, ___

and from this mu-sic I ___ just can't hide.

2. Are you com-ing
4. I've got to

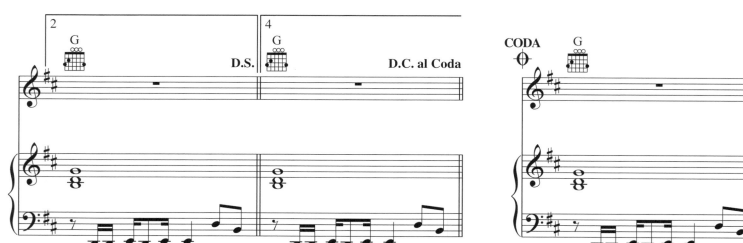

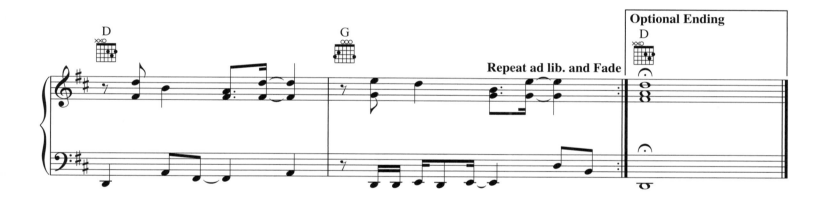

Additional Lyrics

2. Are you coming with me?
   Come, let me take you on a party ride,
   And I'll teach you, teach you, teach you,
   I'll teach you the electric slide.

3. *Instrumental*

4. I've got to move.
   Come, let me take you on a party ride,
   And I'll teach you, teach you, teach you,
   I'll teach you the electric slide.

FIGHT FOR YOUR RIGHT
(To Party)

Words and Music by RICK RUBIN,
ADAM HOROVITZ and ADAM YAUCH

Driving Rock

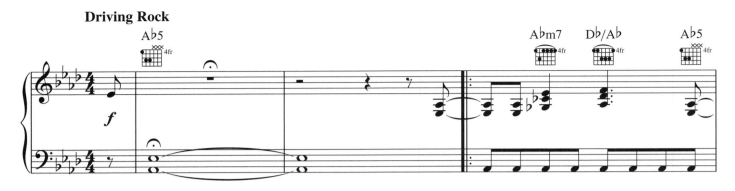

Play 3 times

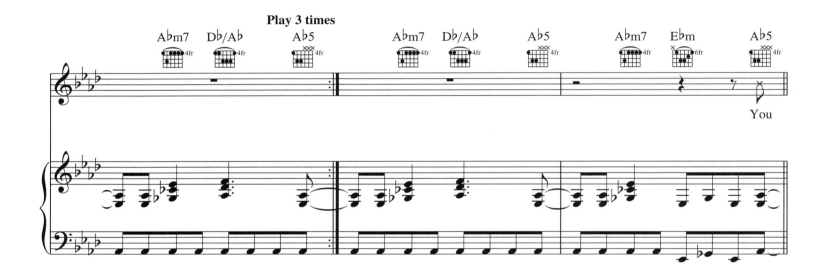

You

wake up late for school, man, you don't wan-na go.
pops _ caught you smok-in', man, he says, "No _ way."

You ask your mom, "please," but she still says no.
That _ hyp - o - crite smokes _ two packs a day.

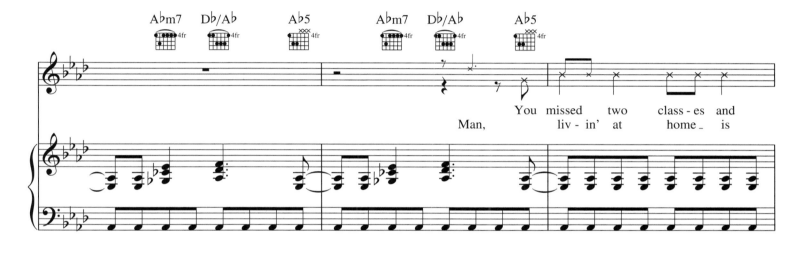

You missed two class - es and
Man, liv - in' at home _ is

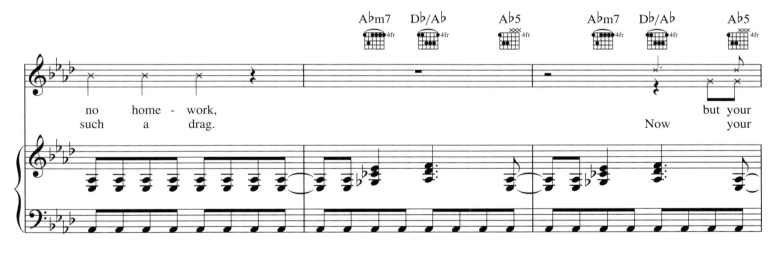

no home - work, but your
such a drag. Now your

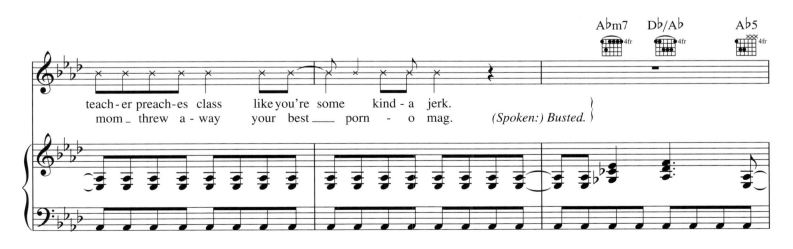

teach - er preach - es class like you're some kind - a jerk.
mom _ threw a - way your best ___ porn - o mag. (Spoken:) Busted.

You got - ta fight _____ for your right _____ to par -

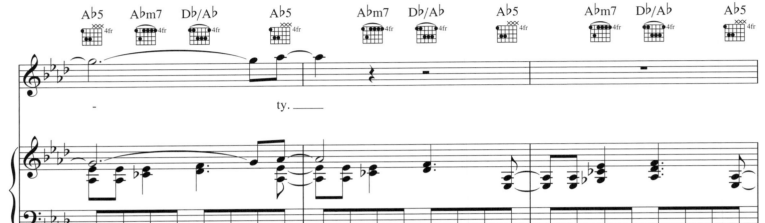

- ty. _____

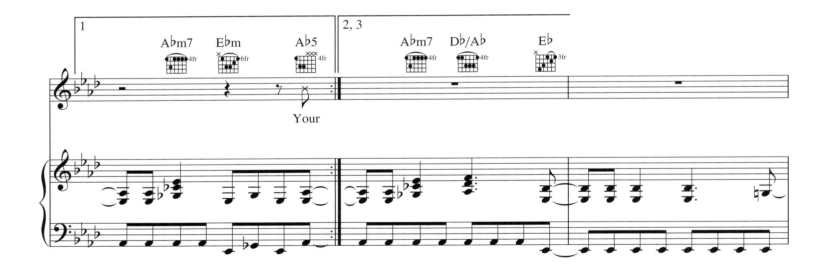

Your

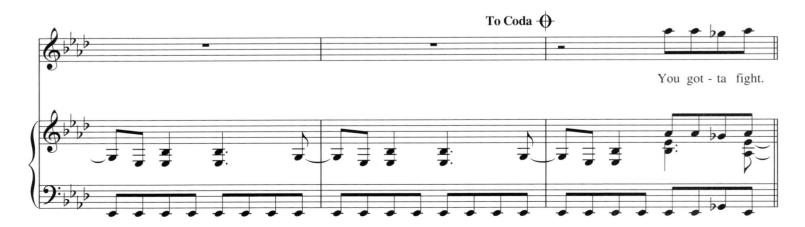

To Coda

You got - ta fight.

Play 3 times

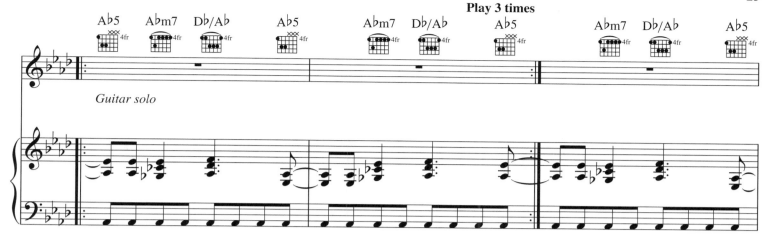

Guitar solo

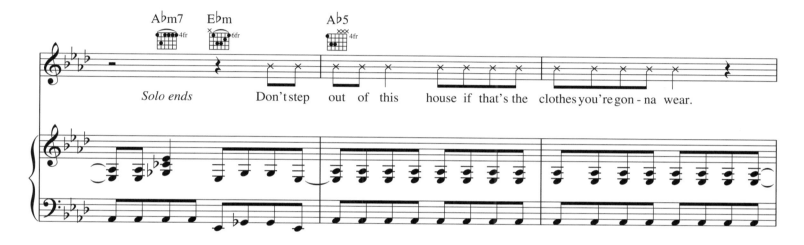

Solo ends Don't step out of this house if that's the clothes you're gon - na wear.

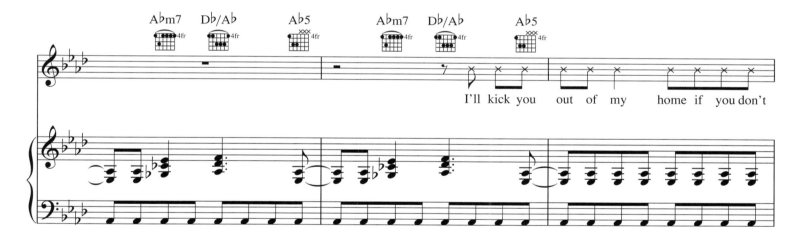

I'll kick you out of my home if you don't

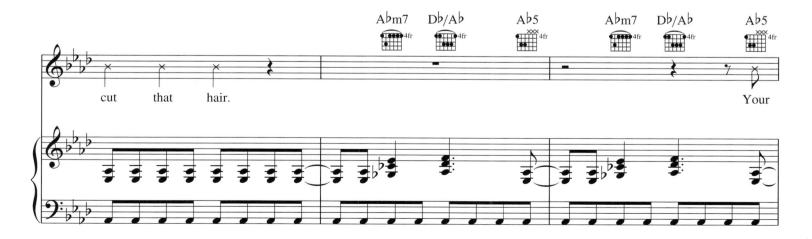

cut that hair. Your

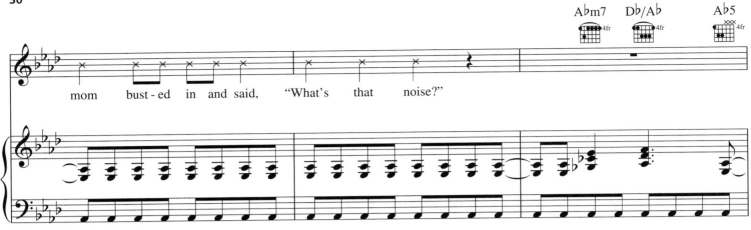

GET DOWN TONIGHT

Words and Music by HARRY WAYNE CASEY
and RICHARD FINCH

Moderate Funk

Ba - by, babe,   let's get to-geth - er   hon - ey, hon - ey,   me and
Ba - by, babe,   I'll meet you;   same place,   same time.

you.   And do the things,   oh,   do the things
Where we can,   oh,   get to-geth - er   and

ease up   that we   like to do.   Oh,
    our   mind.

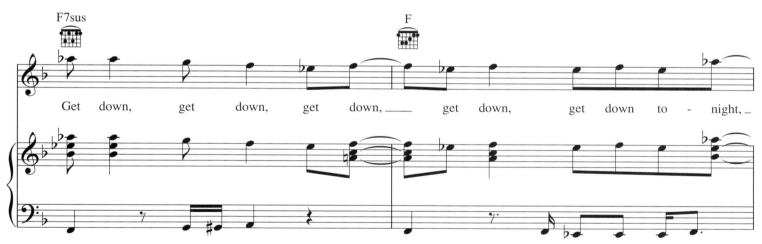

GIRLS JUST WANT TO HAVE FUN

Words and Music by
ROBERT HAZARD

Bright Rock

I come home in the morn-ing light. My moth-
The phone rings in the mid-dle of the night. My fa-
Some boys take a beau-ti-ful girl and hide

-er says, "When you gon-na live your life right?"
-ther yells, "What you gon-na do with your life?"
her a-way from the rest of the world.

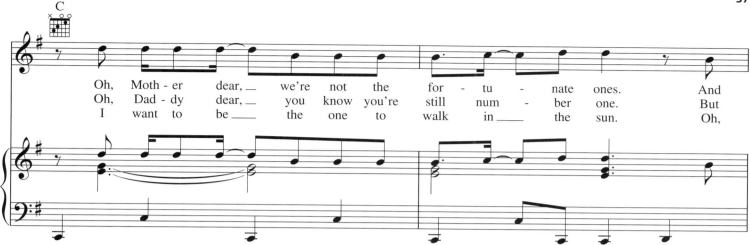

Oh, Moth - er dear, __ we're not the for - tu - nate ones. And
Oh, Dad - dy dear, __ you know you're still num - ber one. But
I want to be __ the one to walk in __ the sun. Oh,

girls,
girls, they want to have fu - un. Oh, __ girls just want to have
girls,

fun. __

girls just want to have... That's all they real - ly want: __

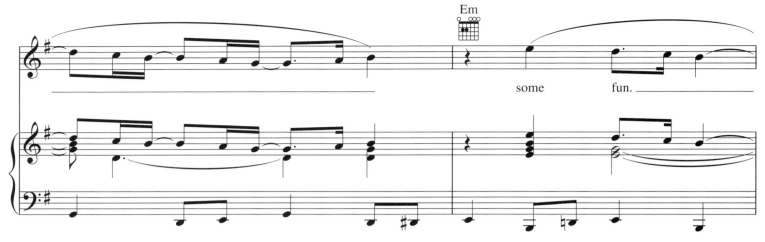

some fun.

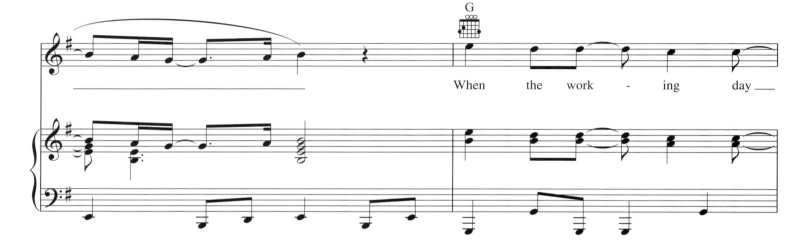

When the work - ing day

is done, oh, girls, they want to have fu -

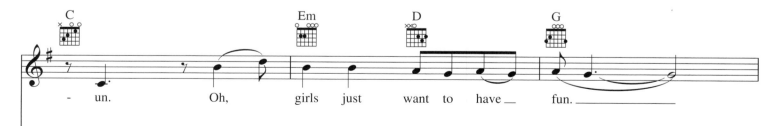

- un. Oh, girls just want to have fun.

HANDS UP
(Give Me Your Heart)

Words and Music by JEAN KLUGER
and DANIEL VANGARDE
English Adaptation by NELLIE BYL

Moderate Rock

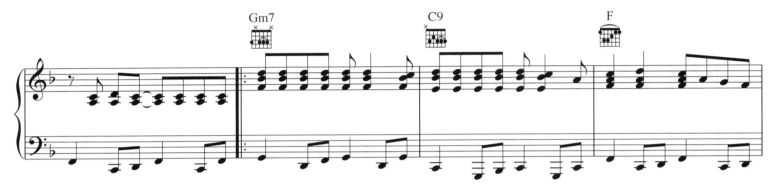

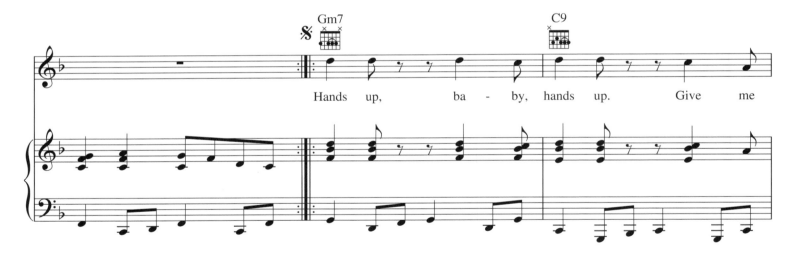

Hands up, ba-by, hands up. Give me

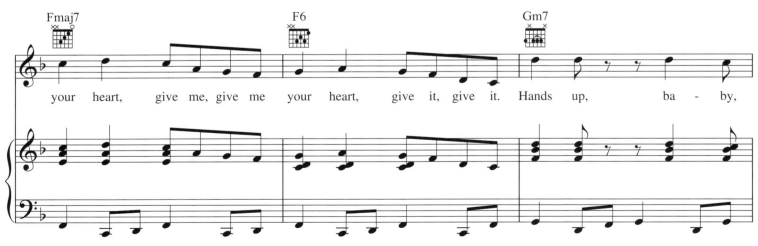

your heart, give me, give me your heart, give it, give it. Hands up, ba-by,

hands up. Give me your heart, give me, give me your heart, give it, give it,

all your love, _____ all your love. _____

An - gel face, __ I love your smile, love your ways, _
With your head __ up in the sky, ev - 'ry day __

I like your style. What can I do __ to get clos - er to you? __
you're walk - ing by. Why don't you ev - er start look - ing at me? __

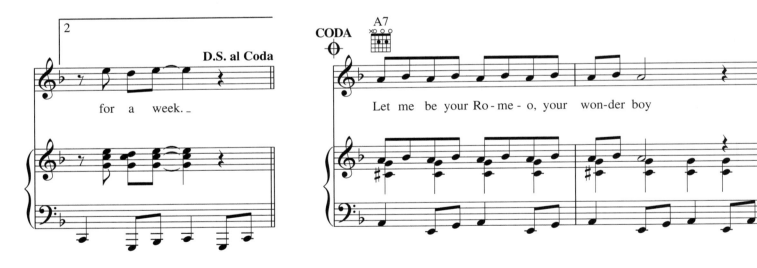

Way for a hol-i-day, for a hol-i-day. Fol-low me, ___

Fol-low me, ___ Why don't you fol-low me? ___ Why don't you fol-low me?

Just come my way, ___ sim-ply kiss me and say: ___ Hands up, ba-by,

Repeat and Fade

hands up. Give me your heart, give me, give me your heart, give it, give it.

THE HOKEY POKEY

Words and Music by CHARLES P. MACAK,
TAFFT BAKER and LARRY LaPRISE

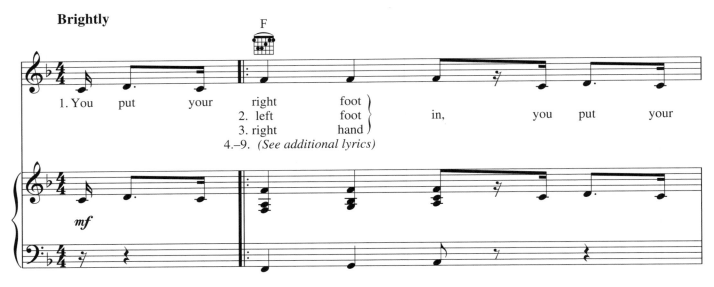

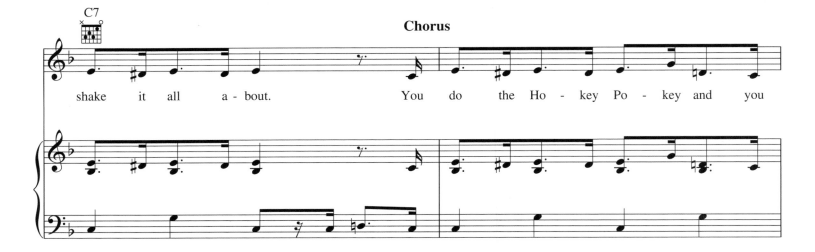

turn your-self a - bout. That's what it's all a -

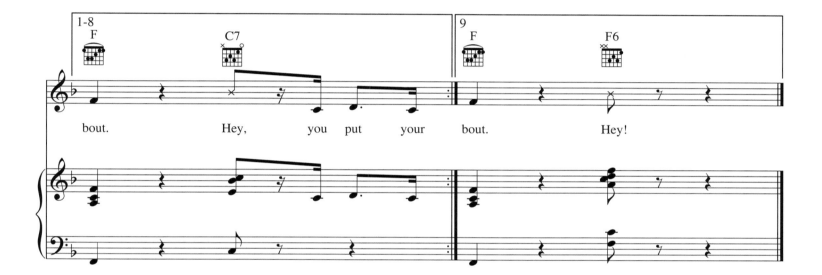

bout. Hey, you put your bout. Hey!

Additional Lyrics

4. Hey, you put your left hand in,
You put your left hand out.
You put your left hand in,
And you shake it all about.
Chorus

5. Hey, you put your right shoulder in,
You put your right shoulder out.
You put your right shoulder in,
And you shake it all about.
Chorus

6. Hey, you put your left shoulder in,
You put your left shoulder out.
You put your left shoulder in,
And you shake it all about.
Chorus

7. Hey, you put your right hip in,
You put your right hip out.
You put your right hip in,
And you shake it all about.
Chorus

8. Hey, you put your left hip in,
You put your left hip out.
You put your left hip in,
And you shake it all about.
Chorus

9. Hey, you put your whole self in,
You put your whole self out.
You put your whole self in,
And you shake it all about.
Chorus

I GOT YOU
(I Feel Good)

Words and Music by
JAMES BROWN

I knew that I would ___ now.
Ah, sug - ar and spice. _____

So good,
So nice,

so good,
so nice,

I got ___ you.
I got ___ you.

Whoa!

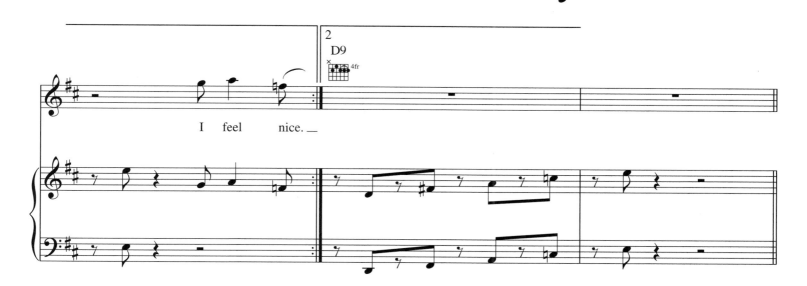

I feel nice. __

I feel _____ nice.

Ah, sug - ar and spice. _____ So nice,

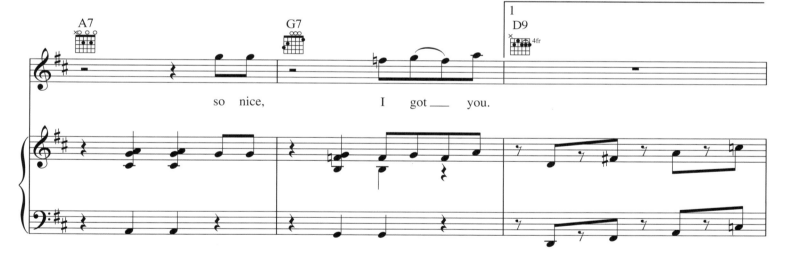

so nice, I got ___ you.

Whoa! I feel good. _

D.S. al Coda
(take 1st lyric)

CODA

So good, so good,

'cause I got ___ you. So good,

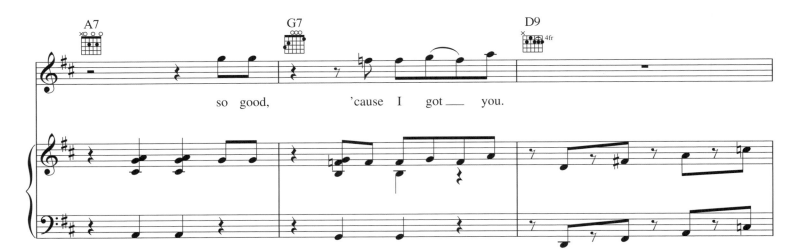

so good, 'cause I got ___ you.

Hey!

rit.

I WILL SURVIVE

Words and Music by DINO FEKARIS
and FREDERICK J. PERREN

Moderate Disco beat

At first I was a-fraid, I was pet-ri-fied; _____ kept think-in'
all the strength I had not to fall a-part; _____ kept try-in'

I could nev - er live _ with-out you by my side. _ But then, I spent so man-y nights think-in'
hard to mend the piec - es of my bro-ken heart. _ And I spent, oh, so man-y nights just feel-in'

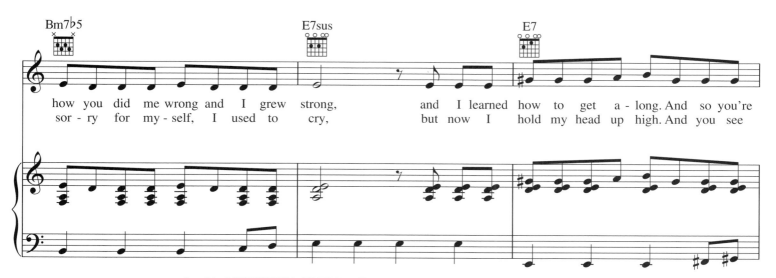

how you did me wrong and I grew strong, and I learned how to get a - long. And so you're
sor - ry for my-self, I used to cry, but now I hold my head up high. And you see

52

Weren't you the one who tried to hurt me with good-bye? Did you think I'd crum-ble, did you think I'd

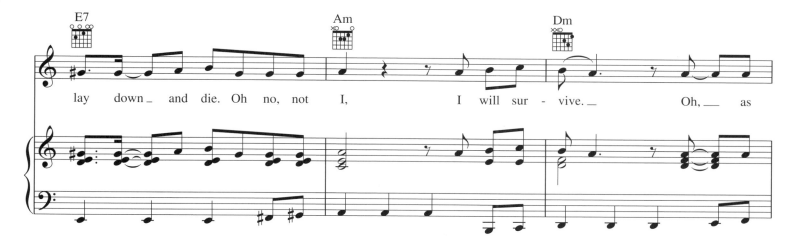

lay down_ and die. Oh no, not I, I will sur-vive. _ Oh, ___ as

long as I know how to love, I know I'll stay a-live. I've got all my life to live, I've got

all my love to give and I'll sur-vive, I will sur-vive! It took vive! Now

I LOVE ROCK 'N ROLL

Words and Music by ALAN MERRILL
and JAKE HOOKER

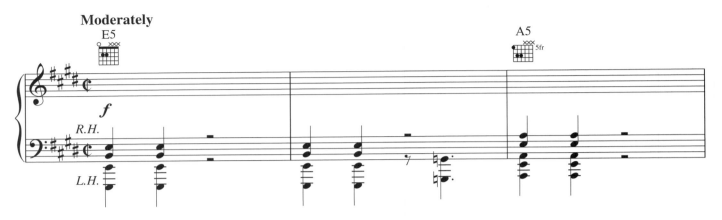

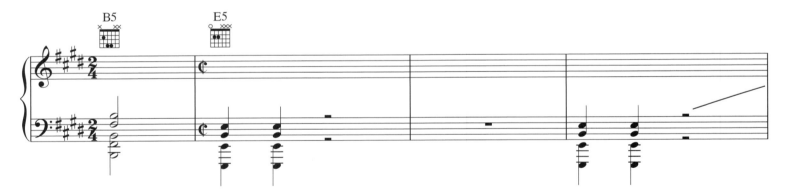

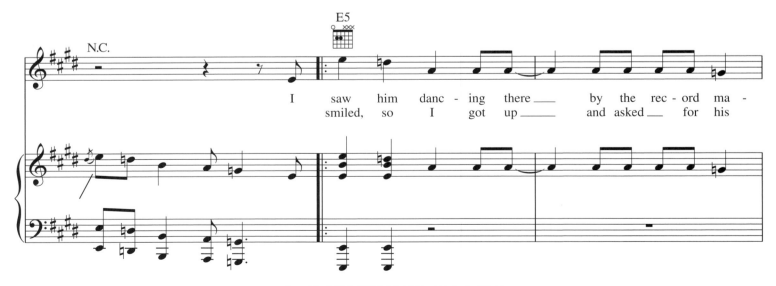

I saw him danc-ing there ___ by the rec-ord ma-
smiled, so I got up ___ and asked ___ for his

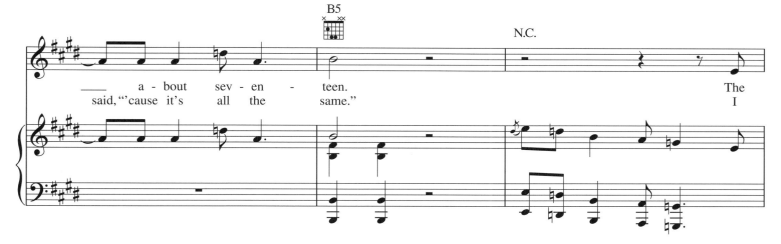

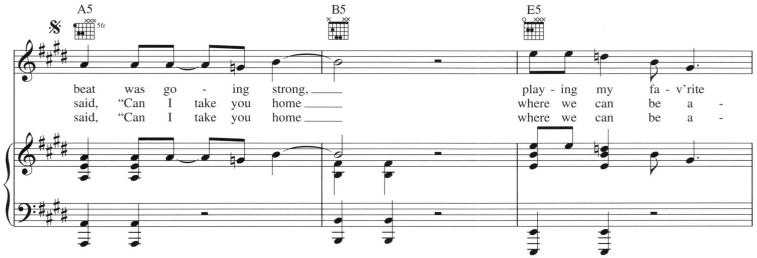

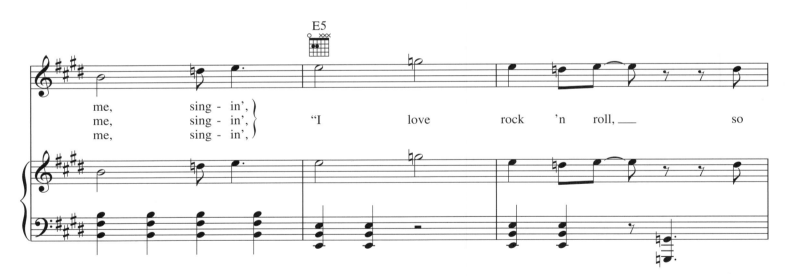

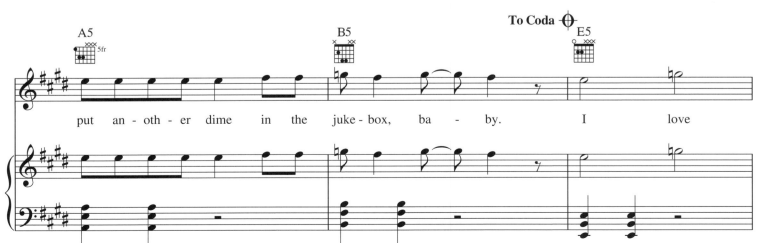

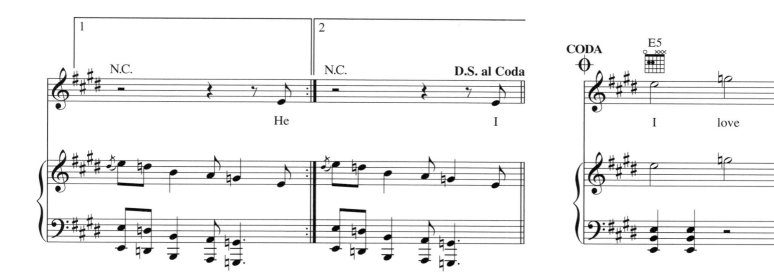

I'M SO EXCITED

Words and Music by TREVOR LAWRENCE,
JUNE POINTER, RUTH POINTER
and ANITA POINTER

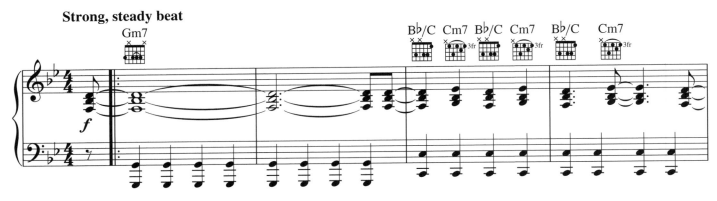

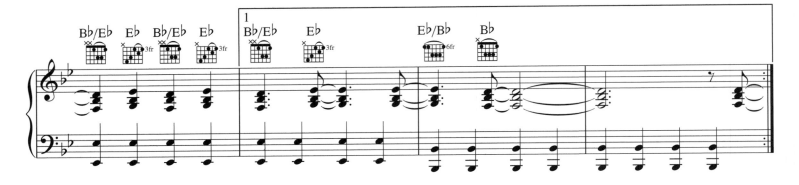

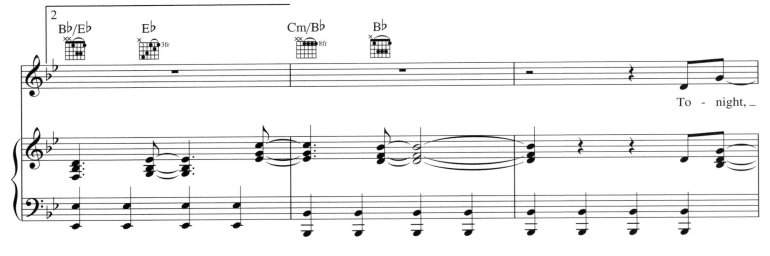

To - night, _ to - night _ we're gon - na make _ it hap - pen,

Instrumental

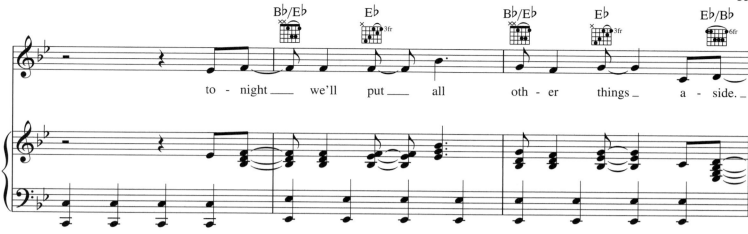

to-night ___ we'll put ___ all oth-er things _ a - side. _

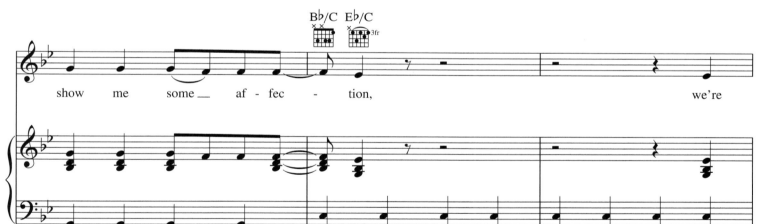

___ Get in _____ this time ___ and

show me some _ af-fec - tion,   we're

go - in' for ___ those pleas-ures in the night. _
Instrumental ends

I want to love you, ___ feel you, ___

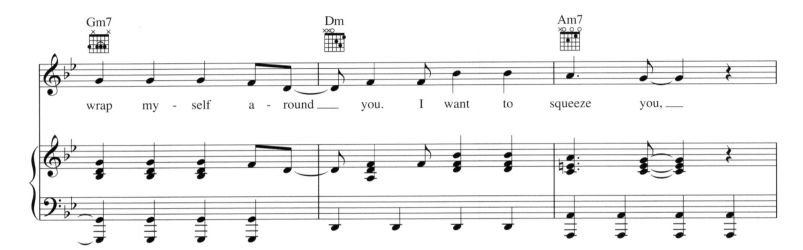

wrap my - self a - round ___ you. I want to squeeze you, ___

please you, ___ I just can't get e - nough. ___ And if ___ you

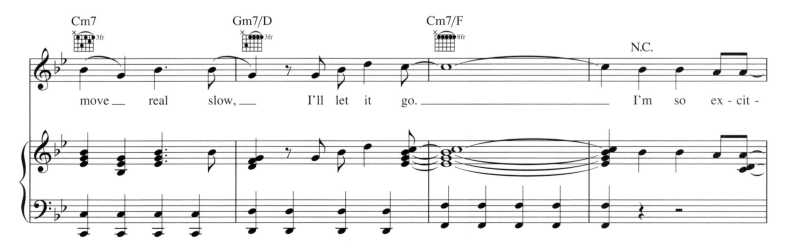

move ___ real slow, ___ I'll let it go. ___ I'm so ex - cit -

- ed, and I just ___ can't hide ___ it.

I'm a - bout to lose con - trol ___ and I think I like ___

___ it! I'm so ex - cit - ed,

and I just ___ can't hide ___ it, and

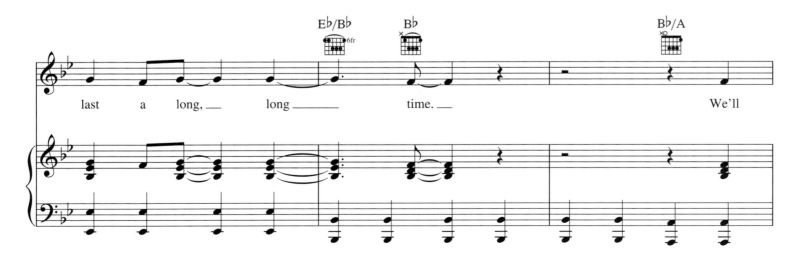

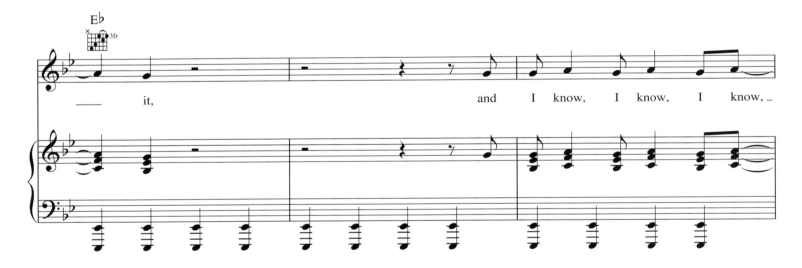

I'M TOO SEXY

Words and Music by FRED FAIRBRASS,
RICHARD FAIRBRASS and ROBERT MANZOLI

Moderate Dance beat

I'm too sex-y for my love, too sex-y for my love. Love's go-ing to leave

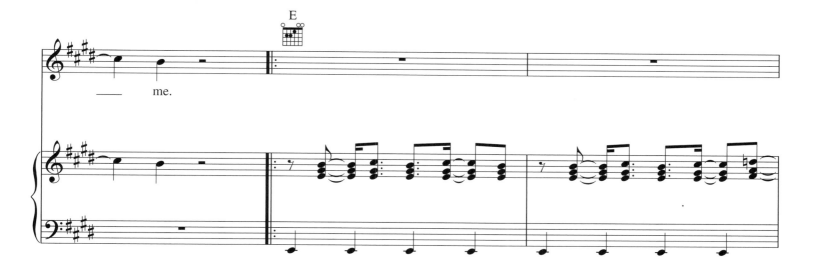

me.

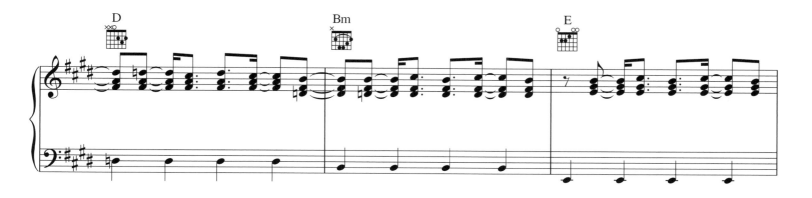

66

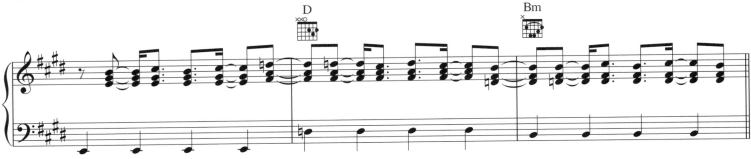

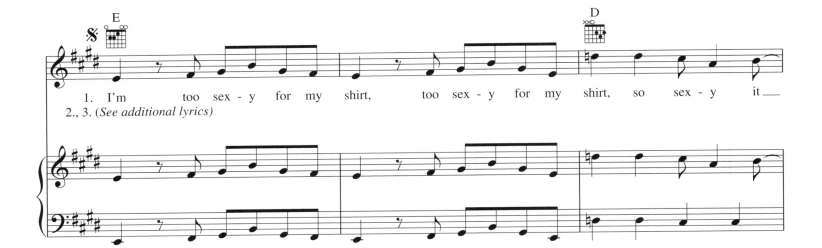

1. I'm too sex-y for my shirt, too sex-y for my shirt, so sex-y it
2., 3. (*See additional lyrics*)

___ hurts, and I'm too sex-y for Mi - lan, too sex-y for Mi -

To Coda ⊕

1st time only

lan, New York and Ja - pan.

my lit-tle turn __ } on the cat-walk. Too sex-y for my,
my lit-tle tush __ }

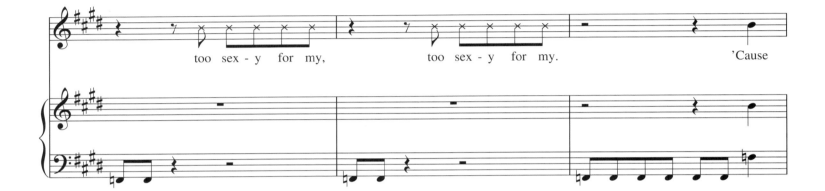

too sex-y for my, too sex-y for my. 'Cause

I'm a mod-el, you know what I mean, __ and I do __ my lit-tle turn __ on the

cat-walk, yeah, on the cat-walk, yeah, the cat-walk. Yeah, __ I shake __

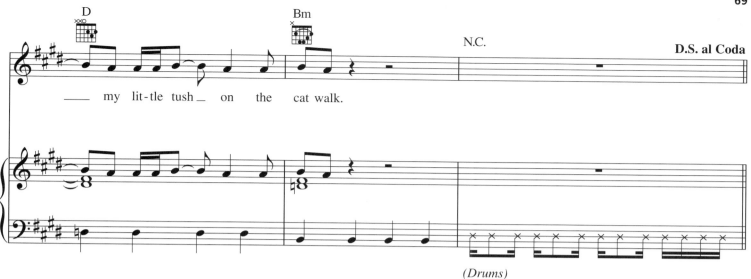

Additional Lyrics

2. I'm too sexy for my car, too sexy for my car,
Too sexy by far.
And I'm too sexy for my hat, too sexy for my hat.
What d'ya think about that?

3. I'm too sexy for my cat, too sexy for my cat.
Poor pussy, poor pussycat.
I'm too sexy for my love, too sexy for my love.
Love's going to leave me.

JOY TO THE WORLD

Words and Music by
HOYT AXTON

wine.
you.
gun.
Sing - ing joy to the world.

All _____ the boys and girls ___ now. Joy to the fish - es in the

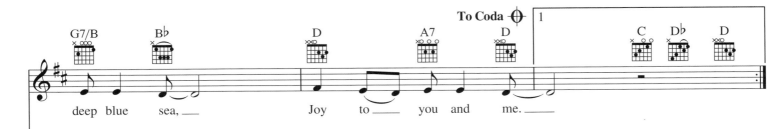

To Coda

deep blue sea, ___ Joy to ___ you and me. ___

D.S. al Coda

You

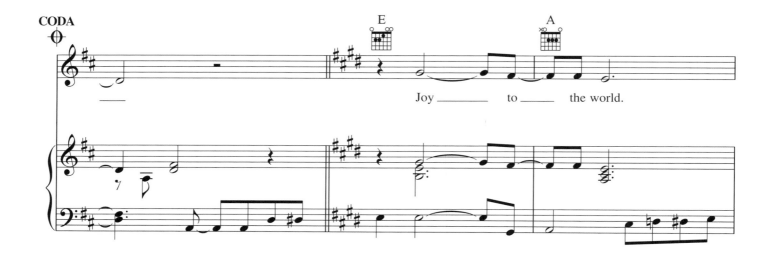

CODA

Joy _____ to _____ the world.

All _____ the boys and girls. _____ Joy _____ to _____

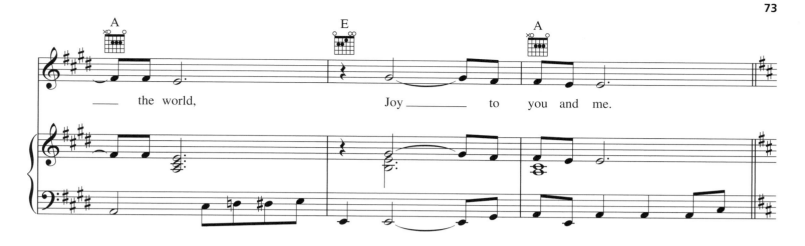

_____ the world, Joy _____ to you and me.

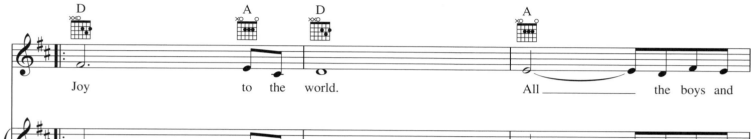

Joy to the world. All _____ the boys and

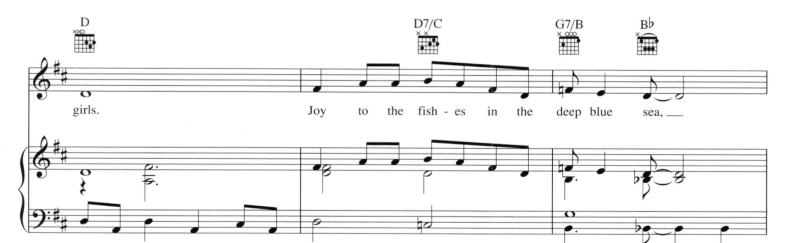

girls. Joy to the fish - es in the deep blue sea, ___

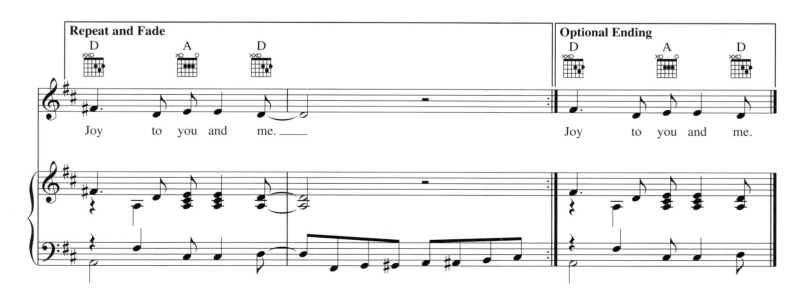

Repeat and Fade

Joy to you and me. ___

Optional Ending

Joy to you and me.

JUMP, JIVE AN' WAIL

Words and Music by
LOUIS PRIMA

Moderately fast Swing

Ba - by, ba - by, it looks like it's __ gon-na hail.

Ba - by, ba - by, it looks like it's __ gon-na hail; You bet-ter

come in - side __ and let me teach you how to jive and wail. __ Oh, __ you got-ta

jump, jive, and then you wail. You got - ta jump, jive, and then you wail. You got - ta

jump, jive, and then you wail. You got - ta jump, jive, and then you wail. You got - ta

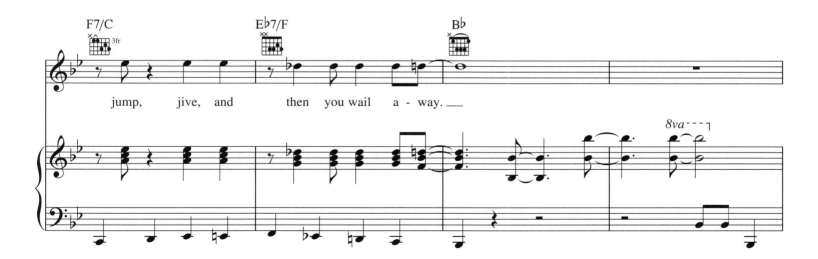

jump, jive, and then you wail a - way. ___

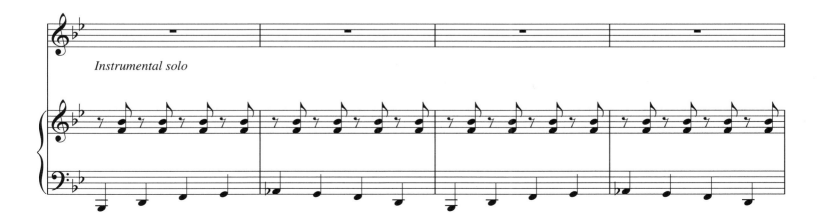

Instrumental solo

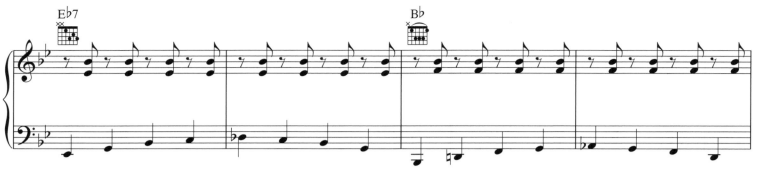

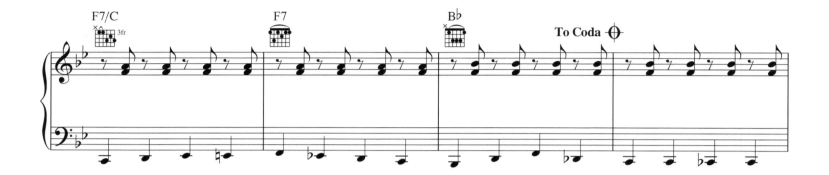

Pa - pa's in the ice - box look - ing for a ____ can of ale.

Pa - pa's in the ice - box look - ing for a ____ can of ale.

Ma - ma's in the back yard

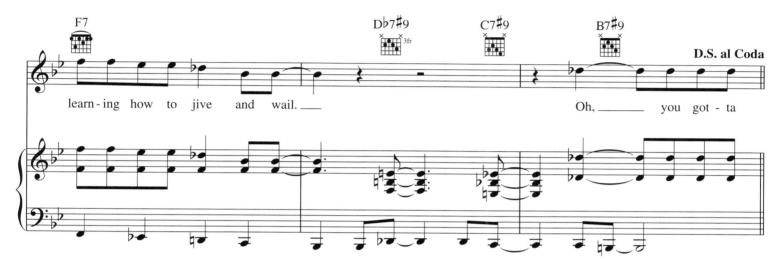

learn-ing how to jive and wail. ___ Oh, ___ you got - ta

D.S. al Coda

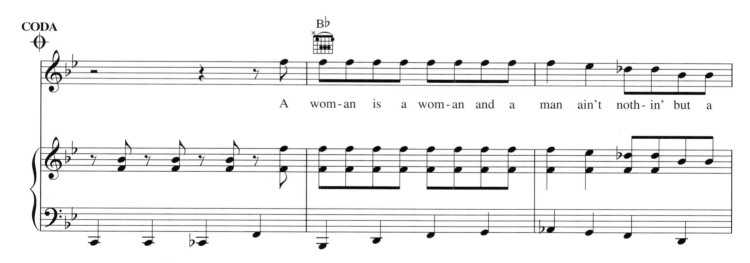

CODA

A wom-an is a wom-an and a man ain't noth-in' but a

male. Wom - an is a wom-an and a

78

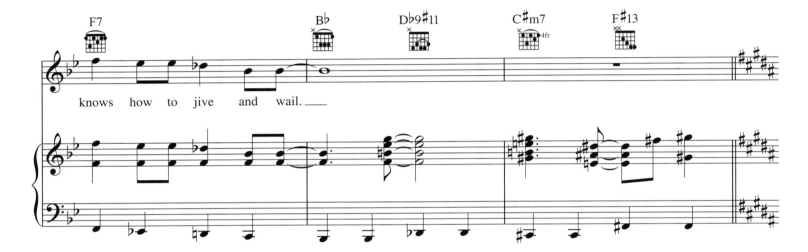

LA BAMBA

By RITCHIE VALENS

Moderate Latin Rock beat

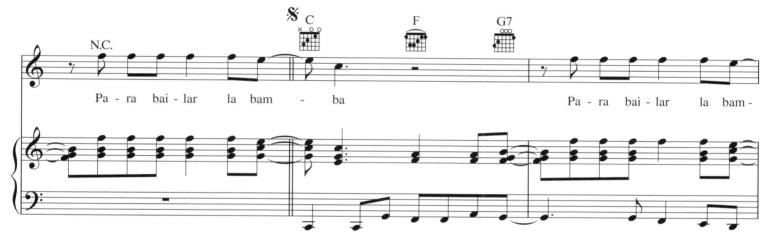

Pa - ra bai - lar la bam - ba   Pa - ra bai - lar la bam -

- ba se ne - ce - si - ta u - na po - ca de gra - cia.

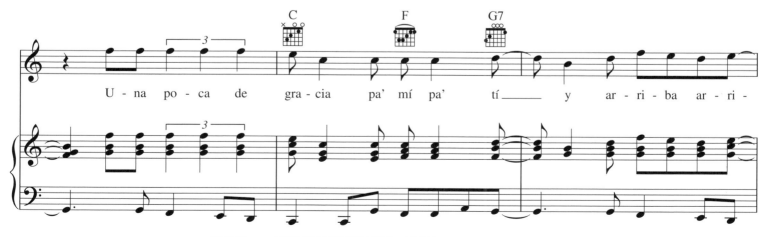

U - na po - ca de gra - cia pa' mí pa' tí____ y ar - ri - ba ar - ri -

-ba;   ar-ri   -ba ar   -ri   -ba por tí se re__

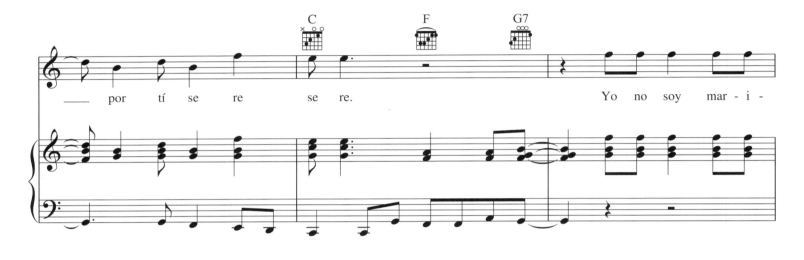

__ por tí se   re se re.   Yo no soy mar-i-

ne-ro.   Yo no soy mar-i   -ne-ro,   soy cap   -i-tán;__

To Coda ⊕

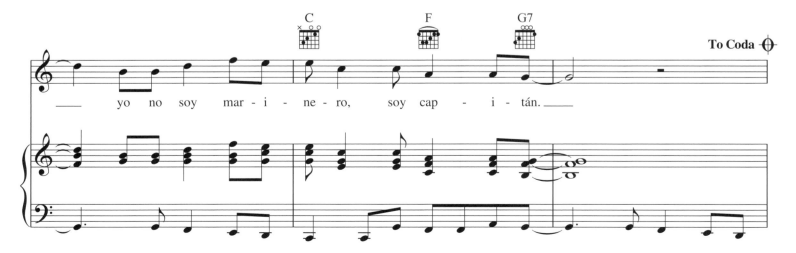

__ yo no soy mar-i   -ne-ro,   soy cap   -i-tán.__

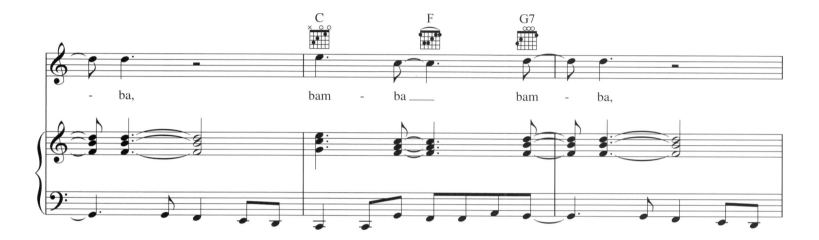

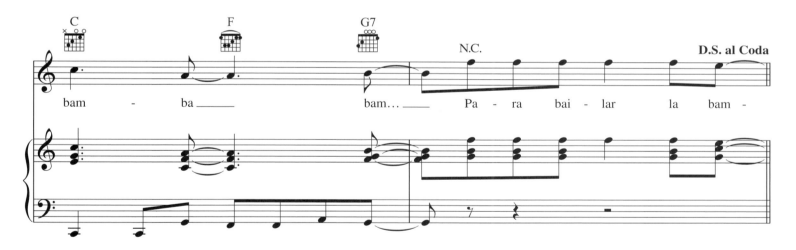

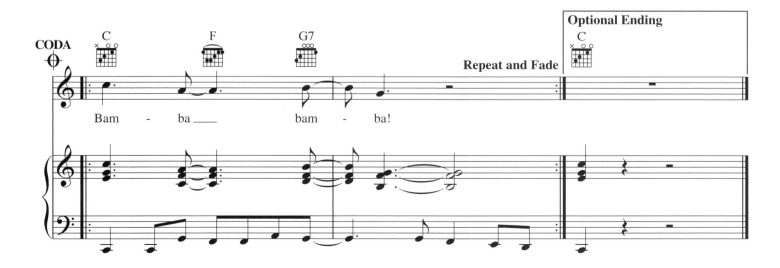

LIMBO ROCK

Words and Music by BILLY STRANGE
and JON SHELDON

Ev - 'ry

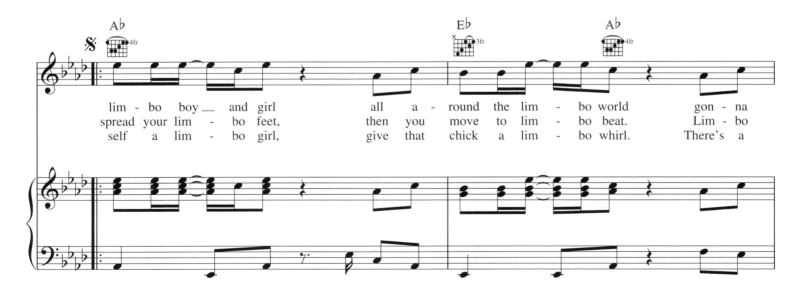

lim - bo boy __ and girl, all a - round the lim - bo world gon - na
spread your lim - bo feet, then you move to lim - bo beat. Lim - bo
self a lim - bo girl, give that chick a lim - bo whirl. There's a

do the lim - bo rock   all a - round the lim - bo block.)
an - kle, lim - bo knee,   bend back like a lim - bo tree.   } Jack be
lim - bo moon _ a - bove,   you will fall in lim - bo love.)

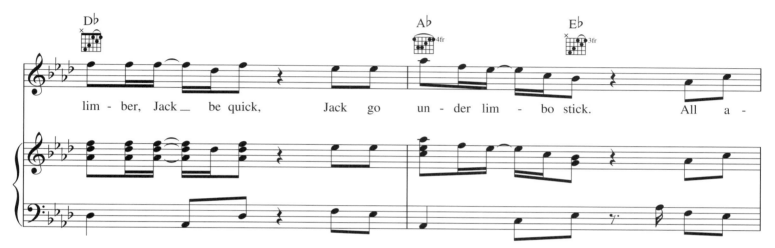

lim - ber, Jack _ be quick,   Jack go un - der lim - bo stick.   All a -

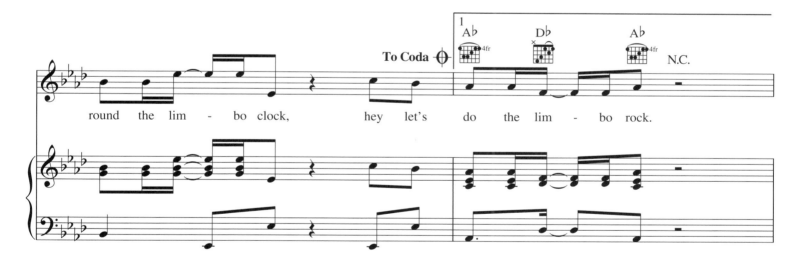

round the lim - bo clock,   hey let's do the lim - bo rock.

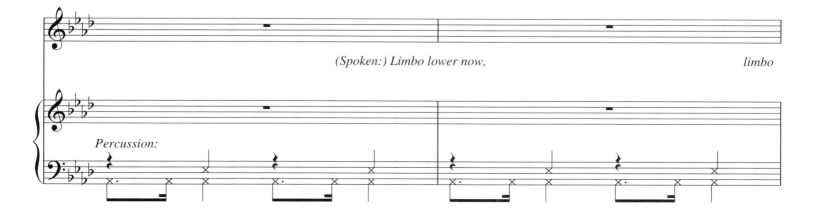

(Spoken:) Limbo lower now,   *limbo*

Percussion:

lower now.   *How low can you go?*   First, you

do the lim - bo rock. La, la, la, la, la, la, la, la; la, la, la,

la, la, la, la, la; la, la, la, la, la, la, la, la; la, la, la,

la, la, la, la, la; la, la, la, la, la, la, la, la; la, la, la,

la, la, la, __ la, la; la, la, la, la, la, la, __ la, la; la, la, la,

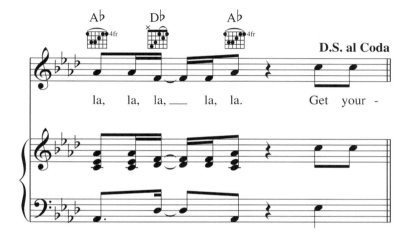

la, la, la, __ la, la. Get your -

D.S. al Coda

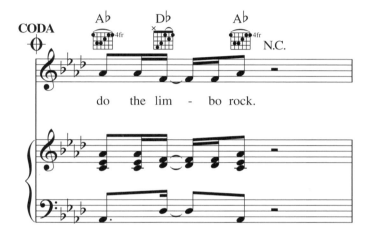

CODA

do the lim - bo rock.

(Spoken:) Don't move that limbo bar. You'll be a limbo star.

Percussion:

How low can you go? La, la, la,

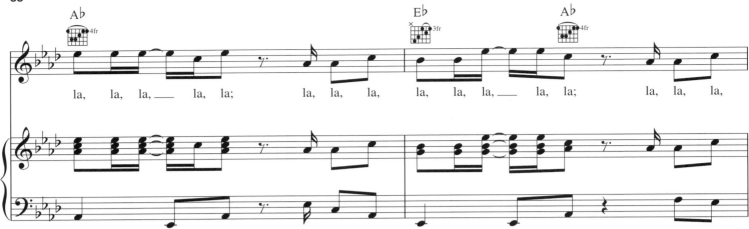

la, la, la, ___ la, la; la, la, la, la, la, la, ___ la, la; la, la, la,

la, la, la, ___ la, la; la, la, la, la, la, la, ___ la, la; la, la, la,

la, la, la, ___ la, la; la, la, la, la, la, la, ___ la, la; la, la, la,

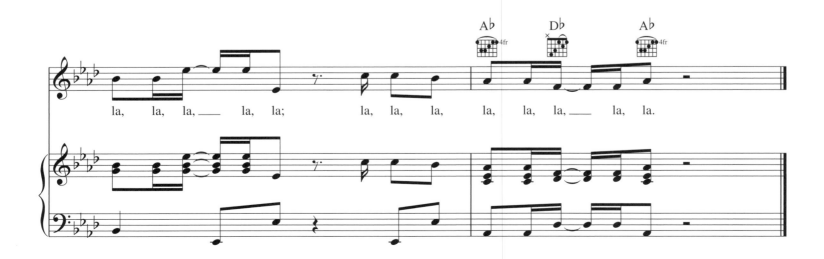

la, la, la, ___ la, la; la, la, la, la, la, la, ___ la, la.

LIVIN' LA VIDA LOCA

Words and Music by ROBI ROSA
and DESMOND CHILD

Fast, with a steady beat

She's in-to su-per-sti-tions, black cats and

voo-doo dolls. __ I feel a prem-o-ni-tion.

That girl's gon-na make me fall. __

She'll make __ you live __ her cra — zy life, __ but she'll take __
Once __ you've had __ a taste __ of her __ you'll nev -

__ a - way __ your pain __ like a bul - let to __ your brain. __
- er be __ the same. __ Yeah, she'll make __ you go __ in - sane. __

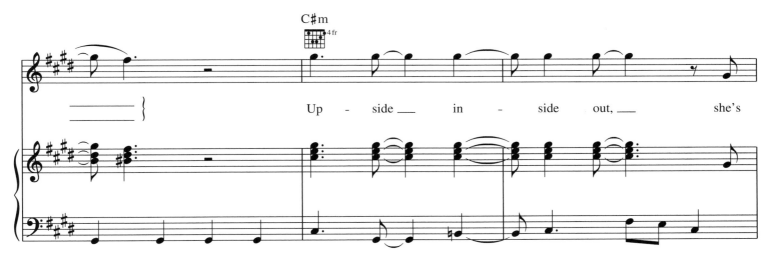

Up - side __ in - side out, __ she's

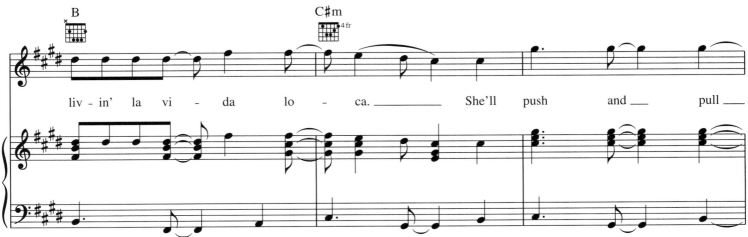

liv - in' la vi - da lo - ca. __ She'll push and __ pull __

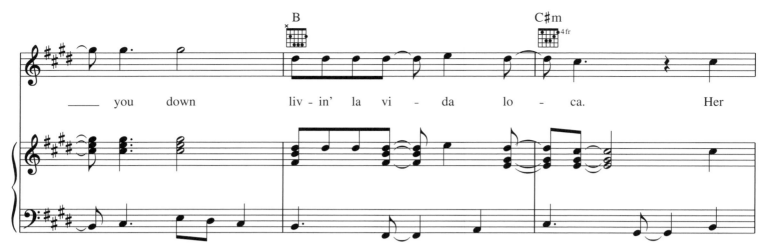

you down liv-in' la vi-da lo-ca. Her

lips are ___ dev-il red ___ and her skin's the col - or of mo -

- cha. She will ___ wear ___ you out ___

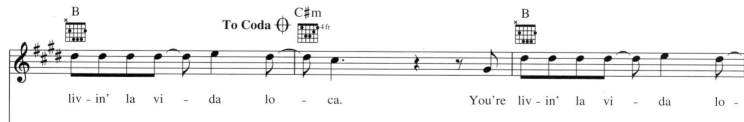

liv-in' la vi-da lo-ca. You're liv-in' la vi-da lo-

-ca. She's liv-in' la vi-da lo-ca.

-ca.

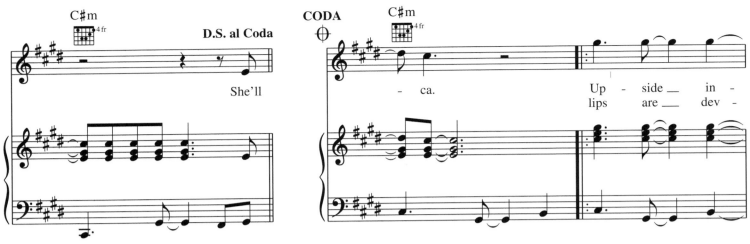

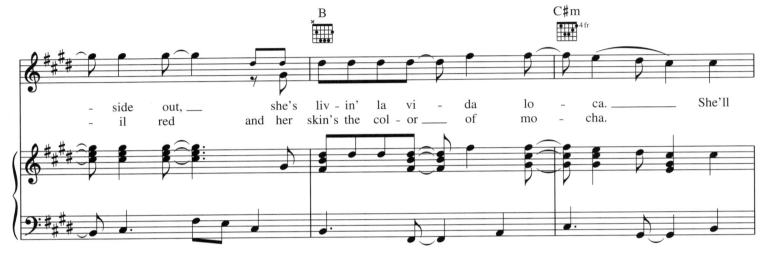

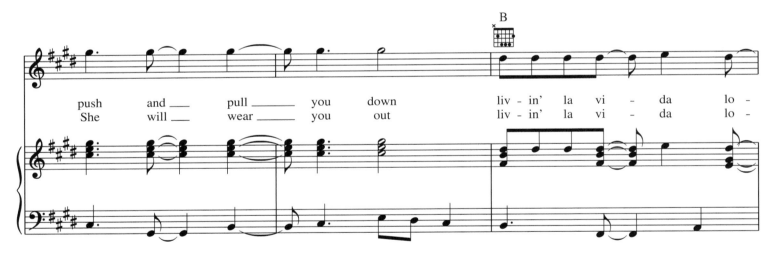

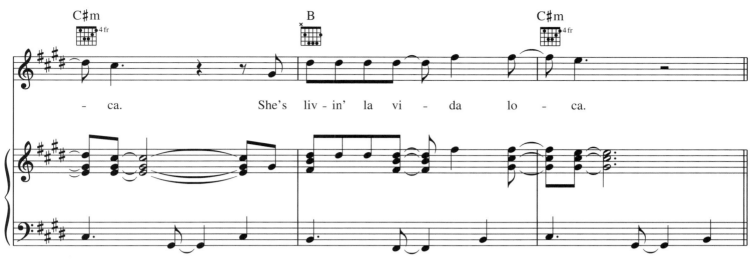

THE LOCO-MOTION

Words and Music by GERRY GOFFIN
and CAROLE KING

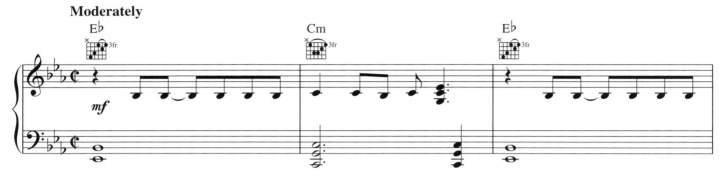

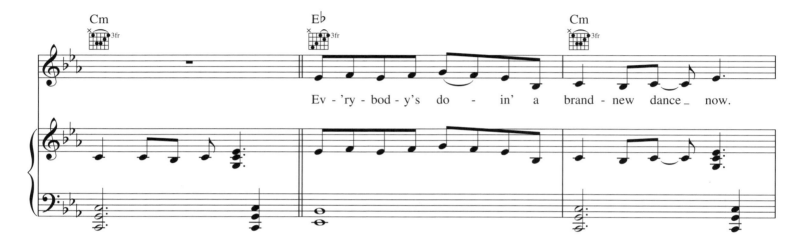

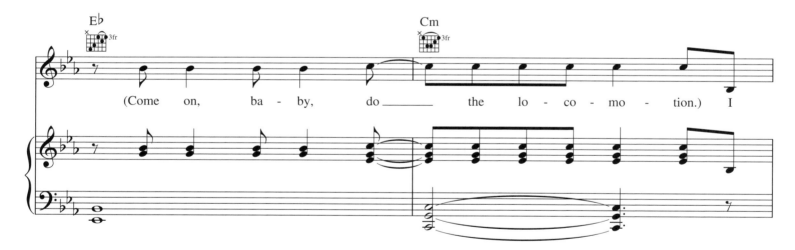

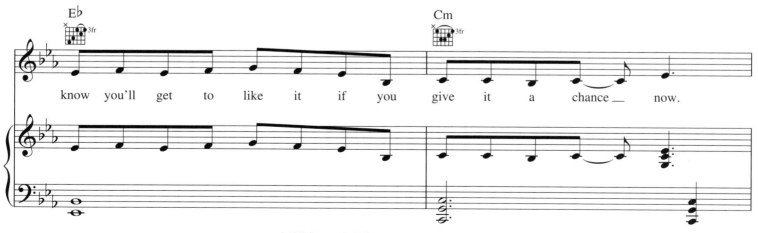

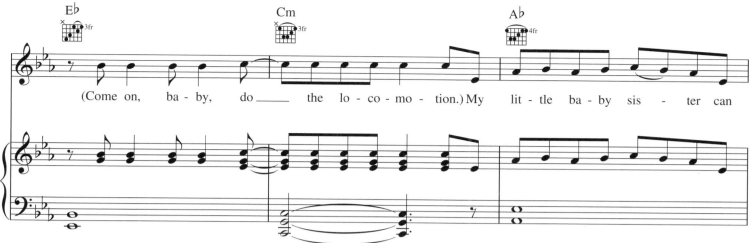

(Come on, ba - by, do ___ the lo - co - mo - tion.) My lit - tle ba - by sis - ter can

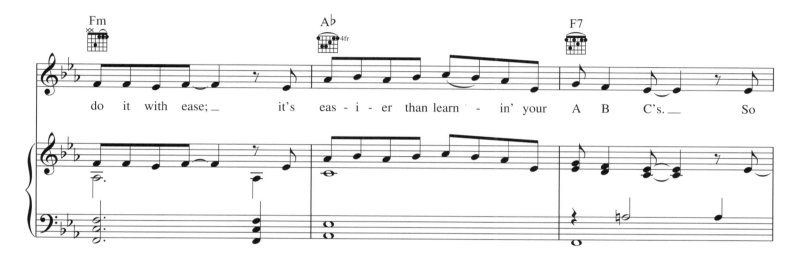

do it with ease; ___ it's eas - i - er than learn - in' your A B C's. ___ So

come on, come on, do ___ the lo - co - mo - tion with me. You got - ta

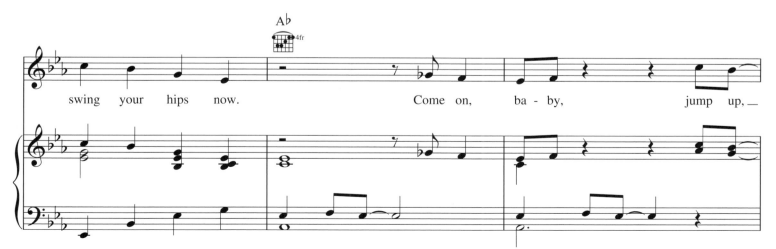

swing your hips now. Come on, ba - by, jump up, ___

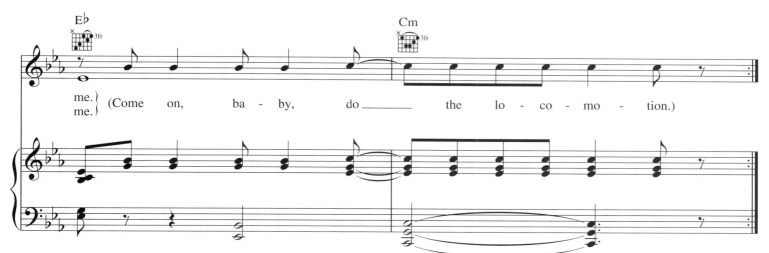

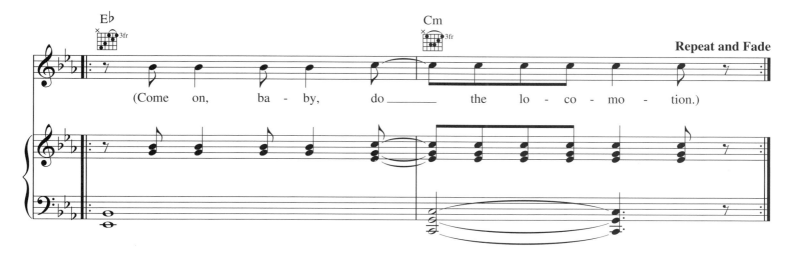

LOUIE, LOUIE

Words and Music by
RICHARD BERRY

Medium Rock beat

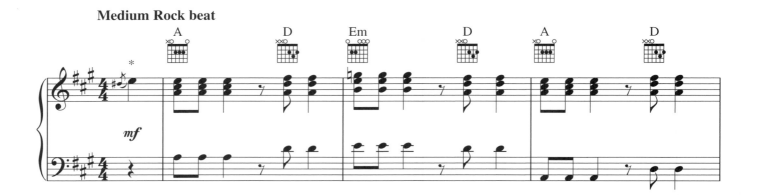

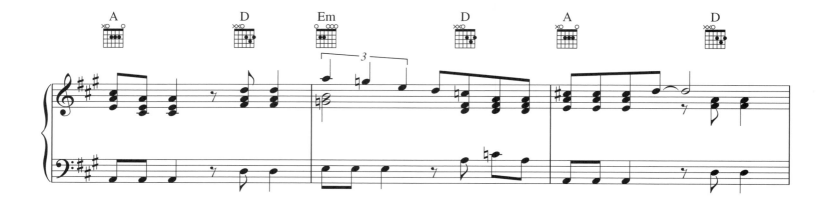

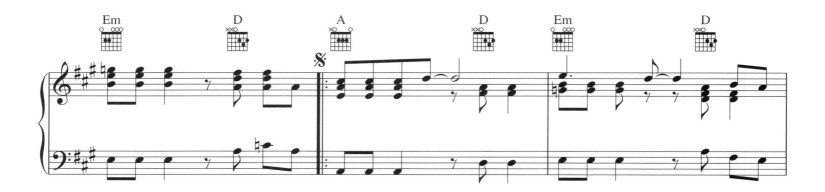

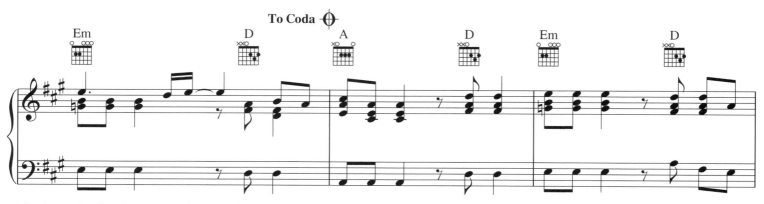

* Lyrics omitted at the request of the publisher.

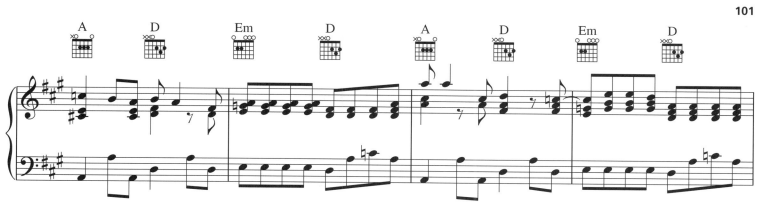

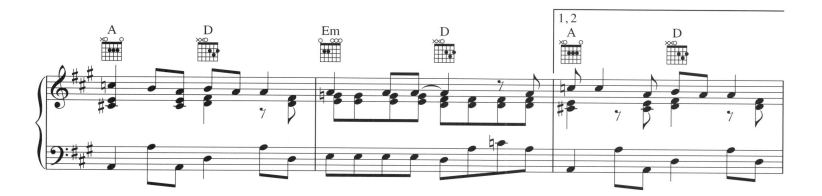

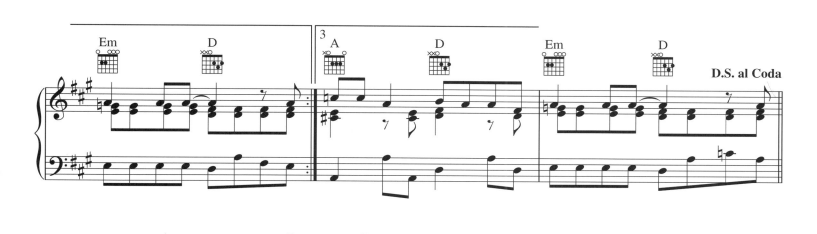

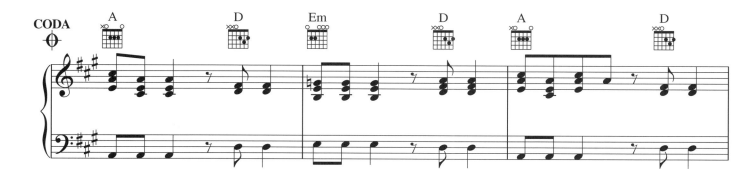

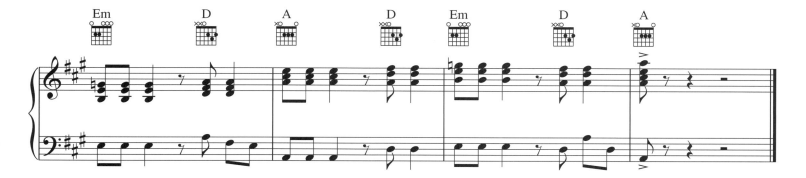

MACHO MAN

Words and Music by JACQUES MORALI, HENRI BELOLO,
VICTOR WILLIS and PETER WHITEHEAD

I've got to be a ma-cho.___

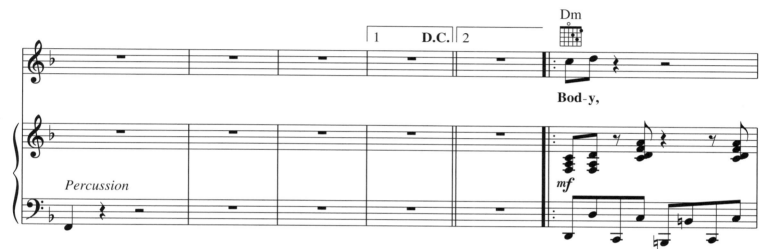

Bod-y,

Percussion

mf

(Last time) **D.S. and Fade on Chorus**

bod-y,   bod-y,   { wan - na feel / gon - na thrill / don't cha stop / it's so hot, }   my bod - y.

(Repeat 4 times)

Additional Lyrics

D.C.   Body, it's so hot, my body,
Body, love to pop my body.
Body, love to please my body.
Body, don't you tease my body.
Body, you'll adore my body.
Body, come explore my body.
Body, made by God, my body.
Body, it's so good, my body.

3. Ev'ry man ought to be a macho man.
To live a life of freedom machos make a stand.
Have their own life style and ideals.
Possess the strength and confidence life's a steal.
You can best believe that he's a macho man.
He's a special person in anybody's land.
Chorus

MAMBO NO. 5
(A Little Bit Of...)

Original Music by DAMASO PEREZ PRADO
Words by LOU BEGA and ZIPPY

cor - ner. The boys say they want some gin and juice, but I real - ly don't wan - na.

Beer bust like I had last week. ___ I must stay deep 'cause talk is cheap. ___ I like

An - gel - a, Pam - el - a, San - dra and Rit - a and as I con - tin - ue you

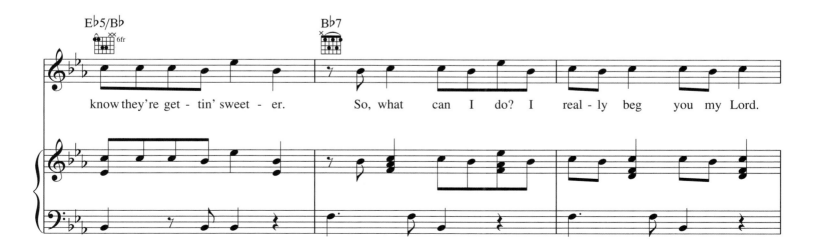

know they're get - tin' sweet - er. So, what can I do? I real - ly beg you my Lord.

To me flirt-in' is just like a sport. An-y-thing fly, it's all good. Let me

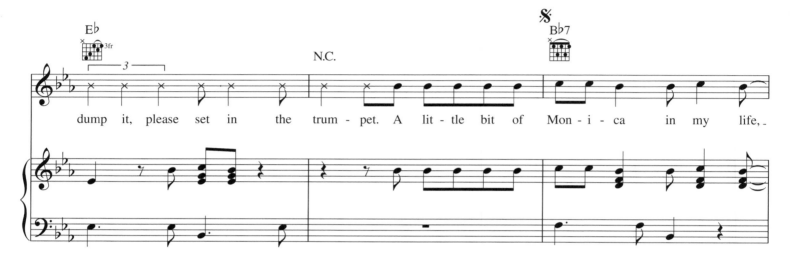

dump it, please set in the trum-pet. A lit-tle bit of Mon-i-ca in my life, __

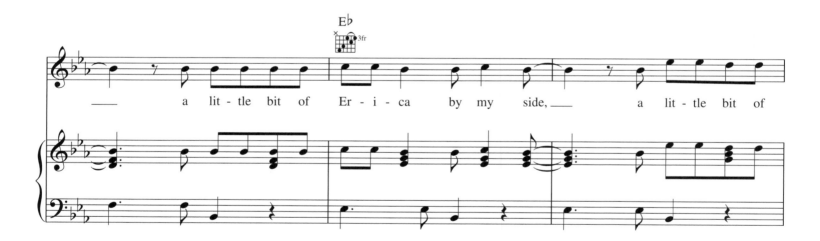

__ a lit-tle bit of Er-i-ca by my side, __ a lit-tle bit of

Rit-a's all I need. __ A lit-tle bit of Tin-a's what I see. __

A lit-tle bit of San-dra in the sun, ___ a lit-tle bit of

Mar-y all night long, ___ a lit-tle bit of Jes-si-ca, here I am, _

___ a lit-tle bit of you makes me your man. ___

Instrumental Five.

Last time (Spoken:) Mambo Number

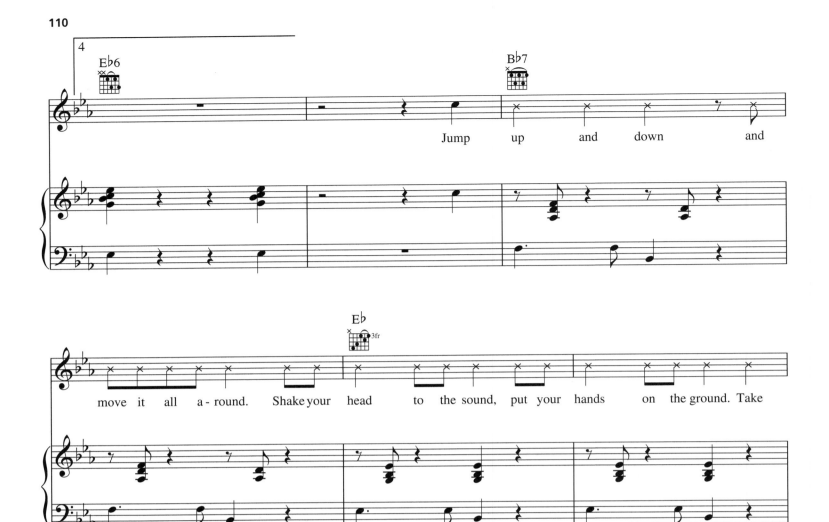

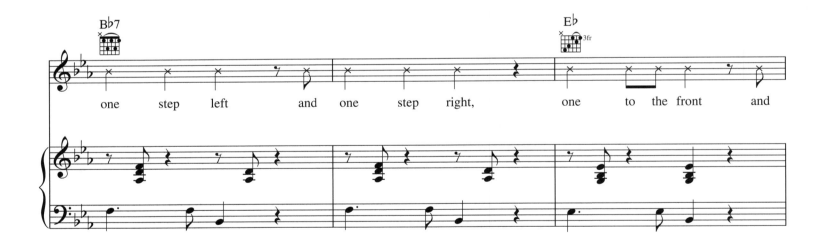

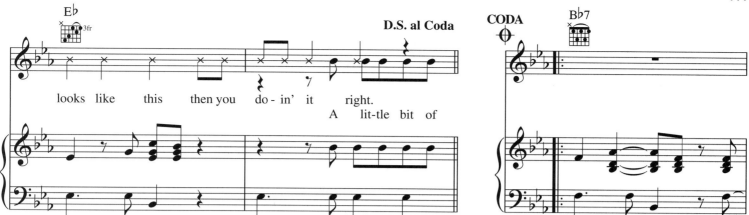

looks like this then you do - in' it right.
A lit-tle bit of

Trum - pet,
(Spoken:) Mambo Number

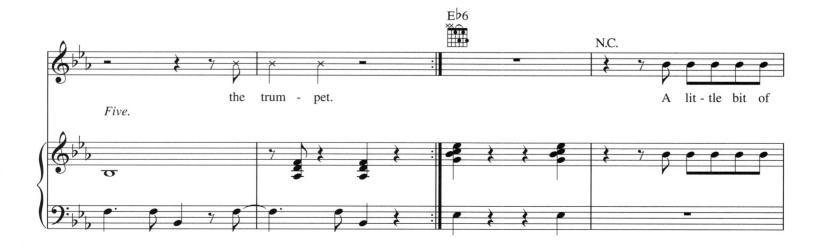

the trum - pet.
Five.
A lit - tle bit of

Mon - i - ca in my life, ___ a lit - tle bit of Er - i - ca by my side, _

___ a lit - tle bit of Rit - a's all I need. ___ A lit - tle bit of

Tin - a's what I see. ___ A lit - tle bit of San - dra in the sun, ___ a lit - tle bit of

Mar - y all night long, ___ a lit - tle bit of Jes - si - ca, here I am, _

Last time (Spoken:) Mambo Number

MONSTER MASH

Words and Music by BOBBY PICKETT
and LEONARD CAPIZZI

116

Easy, Igor, you impetuous young boy.

Additional Lyrics

2. *From my laboratory in the castle east,*
   To the master bedroom where the vampires feast,
   The ghouls all came from their humble abodes
   To get a jolt from my electrodes.
   (to Chorus: They did the mash)

3. *The scene was rockin'. All were digging the sounds.*
   Igor on chains, backed by his baying hounds.
   The coffin-bangers were about to arrive
   With their vocal group, "The Crypt-Kicker Five."
   (to Chorus: They played the mash)

4. *Out from his coffin, Drac's voice did ring.*
   Seems he was troubled by just one thing.
   He opened the lid and shook his fist,
   And said, "Whatever happened to my Transylvanian Twist?"
   (to Chorus: It's now the mash)

5. *Now everything's cool, Drac's a part of the band.*
   And my monster mash is the hit of the land.
   For you, the living, this mash was meant, too,
   When you get to my door, tell them Boris sent you.
   (to Chorus: Then you can mash)

MONY, MONY

Words and Music by BOBBY BLOOM,
TOMMY JAMES, RITCHIE CORDELL
and BO GENTRY

Here she comes now, say, Mo - ny, Mo - ny.
Wake me, shake me, Mo - ny, Mo - ny.

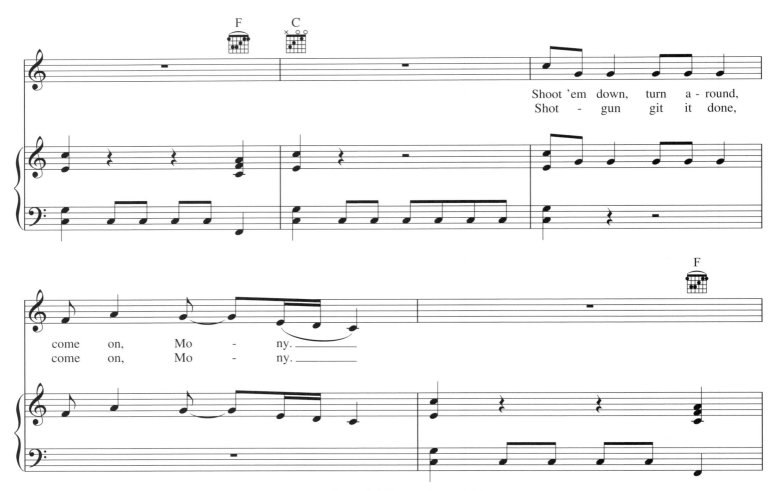

Shoot 'em down, turn a - round,
Shot - gun git it done,

come on, Mo - ny.
come on, Mo - ny.

Hey, she give me lov - in', I feel ____ all right, _ now. ____
Don't stop cook - in', it feels ____ so good, _ yeah. ____

You've got me

toss - in', turn - in' the mid - dle of the night, and I feel ____
Don't stop now. Come on, Mo - ny.

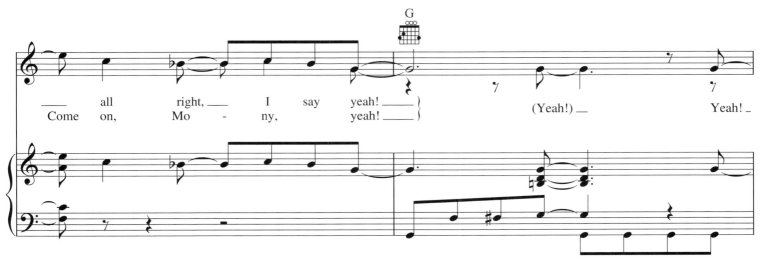

____ all right, ____ I say yeah! ____ (Yeah!) ____ Yeah! _
Come on, Mo - ny, yeah!

(Yeah!) Yeah! (Yeah!) Yeah! (Yeah!) Yeah!

(Yeah!) Yeah! You make me feel (Mo - ny, Mo - ny)

so (Mo - ny, Mo - ny) good. (Mo - ny, Mo - ny) Yeah! (Mo - ny, Mo - ny)

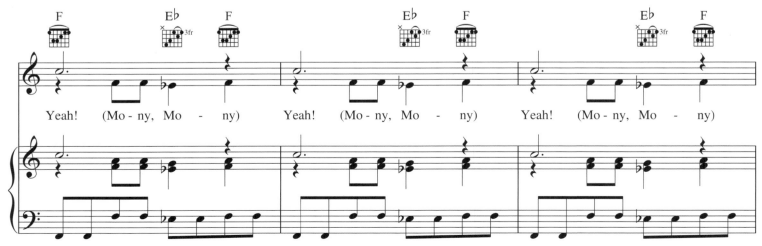

Yeah! (Mo - ny, Mo - ny) Yeah! (Mo - ny, Mo - ny) Yeah! (Mo - ny, Mo - ny)

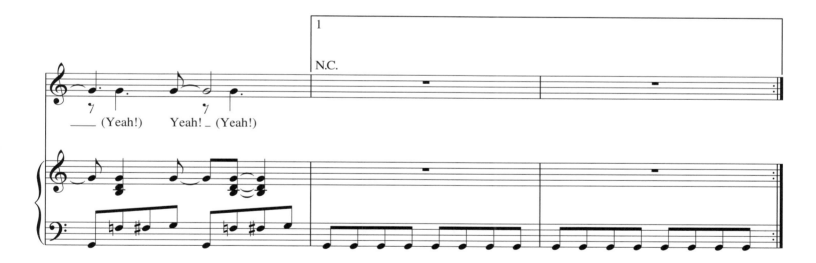

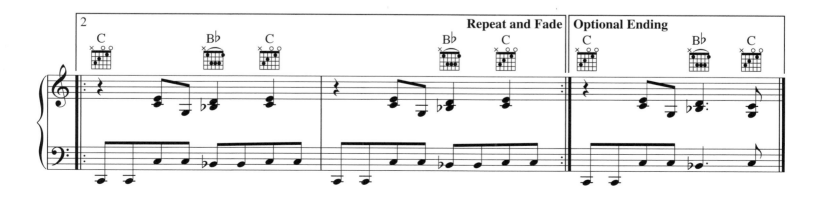

MY SHARONA

Words and Music by DOUG FIEGER
and BERTON AVERRE

Fast Rock

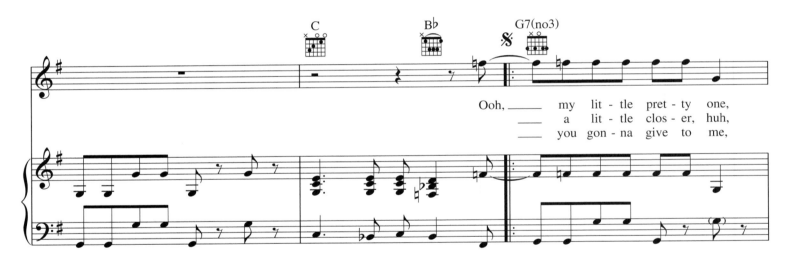

Ooh, _____ my lit - tle pret - ty one,
_____ a lit - tle clos - er, huh,
_____ you gon - na give to me,

my pret - ty one.   When _____ you gon - na give me some time, Sha - ro - na?   Ooh, _____
a - will ya, huh?   Close _____ e - nough to look in my eyes, Sha - ro - na.   Keep -
g - give to me?   Is _____ it just a mat - ter of time, Sha - ro - na?   Is

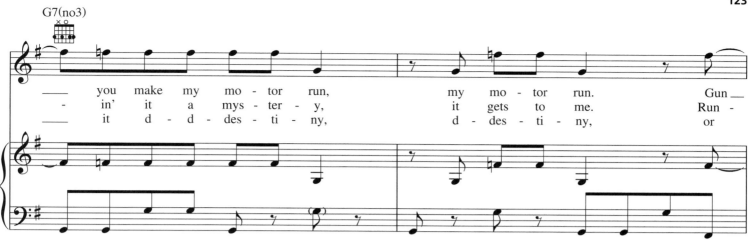

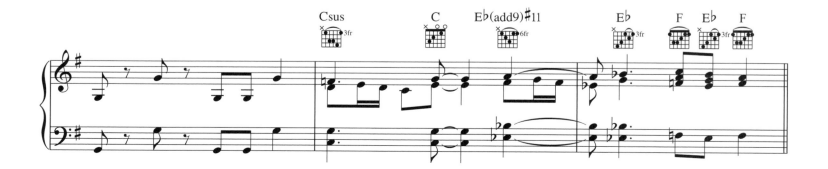

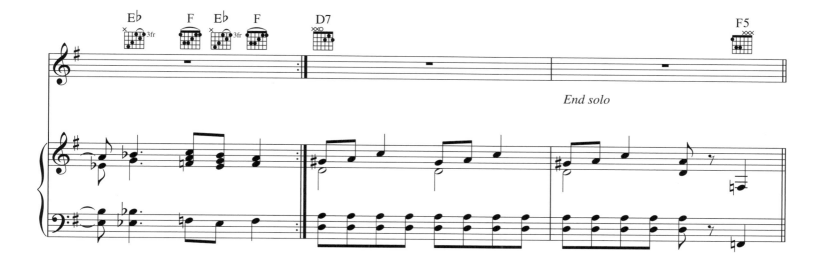

End solo

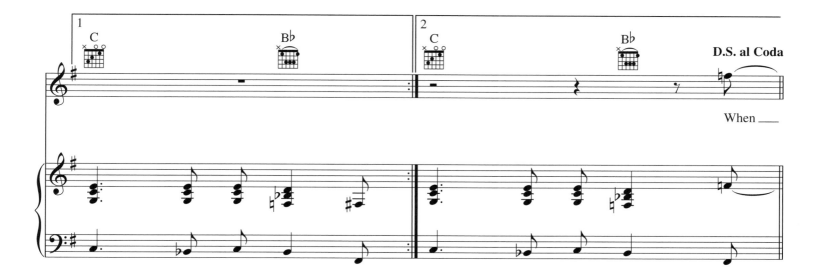

D.S. al Coda

When ___

126

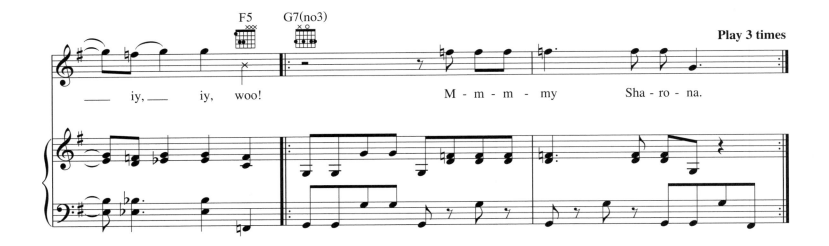

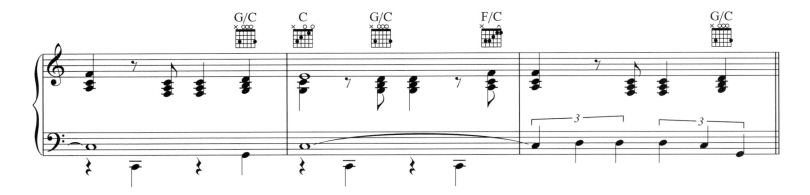

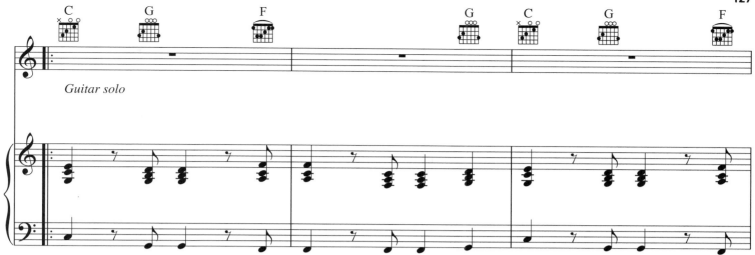

Guitar solo

Repeat ad lib.

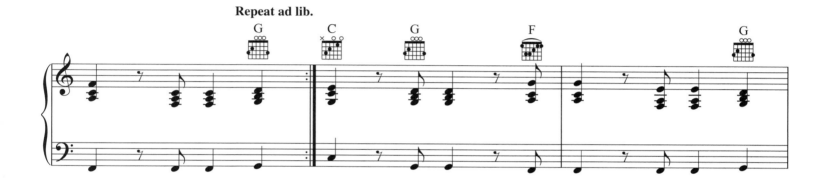

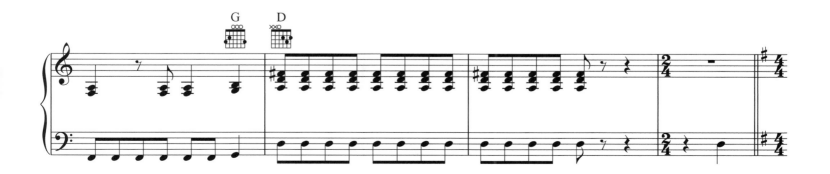

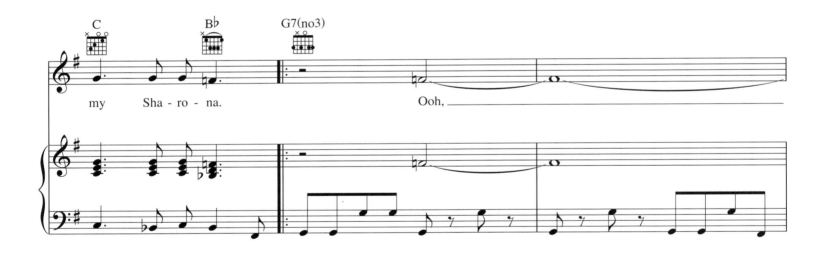

ROCK & ROLL - PART II
(The Hey Song)

Words and Music by MIKE LEANDER
and GARY GLITTER

Heavy Rock Shuffle

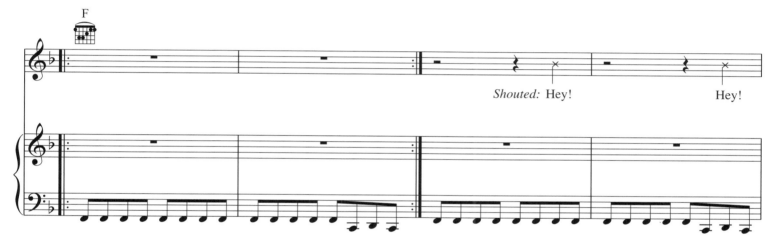

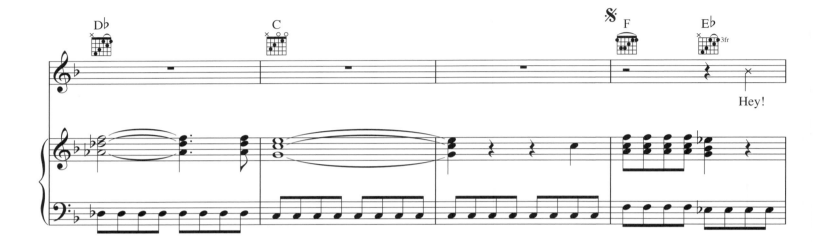

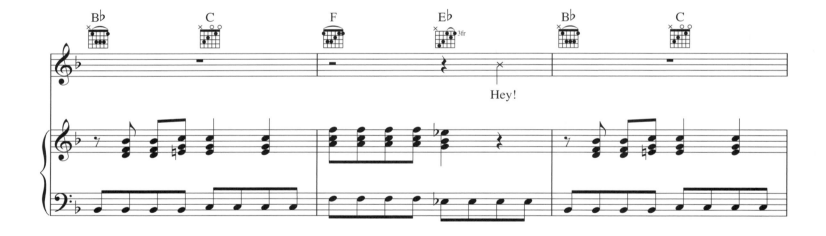

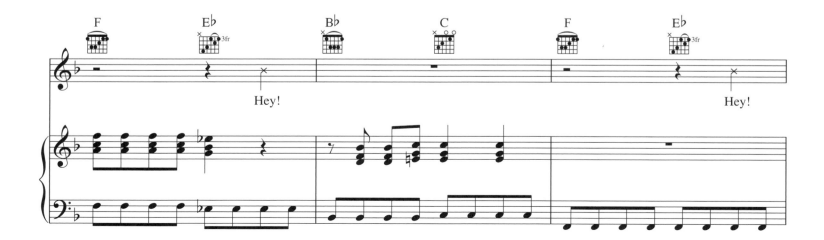

ROCK AND ROLL ALL NITE

Words and Music by PAUL STANLEY
and GENE SIMMONS

Moderately fast Rock

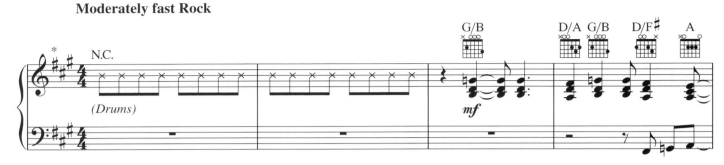

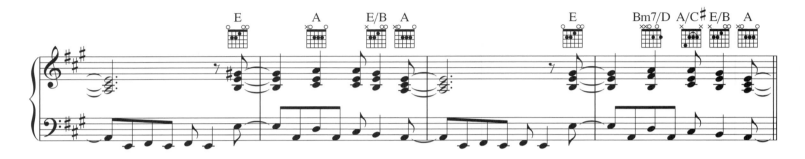

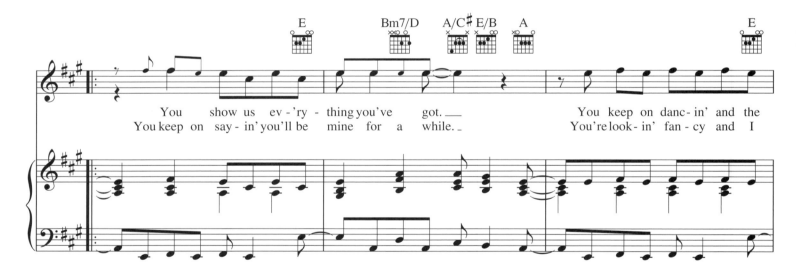

You show us ev - 'ry - thing you've got. ___ You keep on danc - in' and the
You keep on say - in' you'll be mine for a while. ___ You're look - in' fan - cy and I

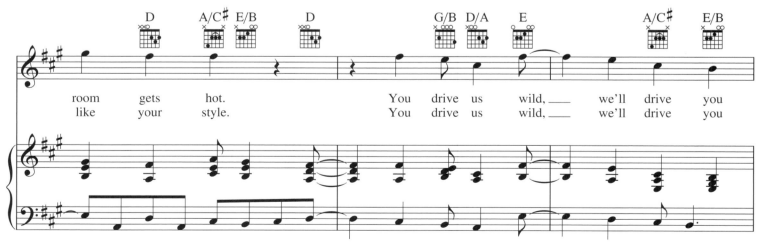

room gets hot. You drive us wild, ___ we'll drive you
like gets your style. You drive us wild, ___ we'll drive you

*Recorded a half step lower.

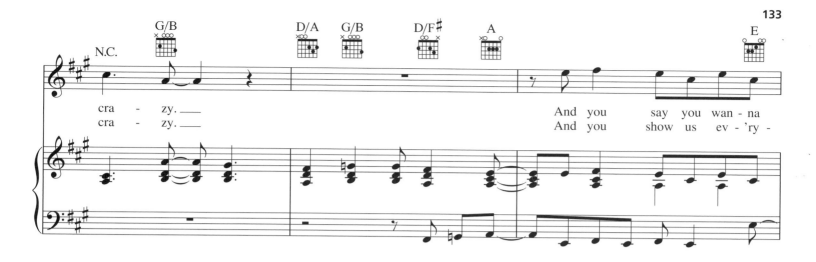

cra - zy. ___
cra - zy. ___

And you say you wan - na
And you show us ev - 'ry -

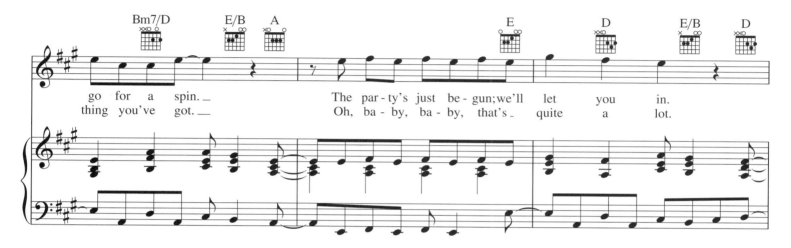

go for a spin. ___
thing you've got. ___

The par - ty's just be - gun; we'll let you in.
Oh, ba - by, ba - by, that's ___ quite a lot.

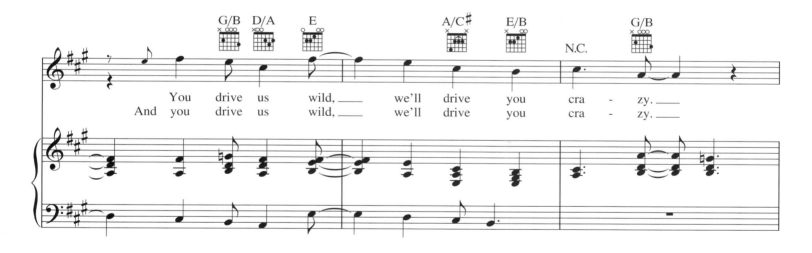

You drive us wild, ___ we'll drive you cra - zy. ___
And you drive us wild, ___ we'll drive you cra - zy. ___

You keep on shout - in', you ___ keep on shout - in'.)
You keep on shout - in', you ___ keep on shout - in'.)

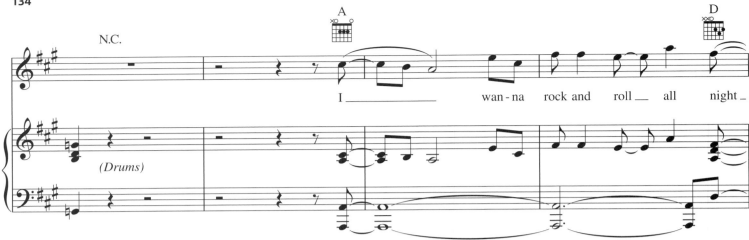

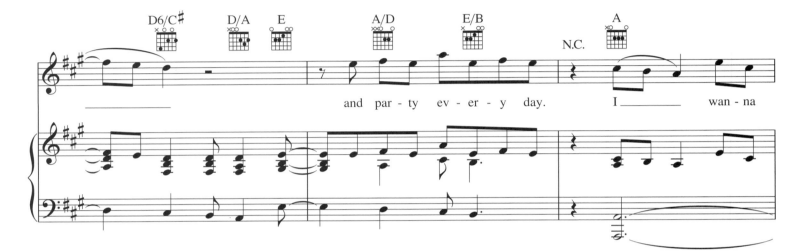

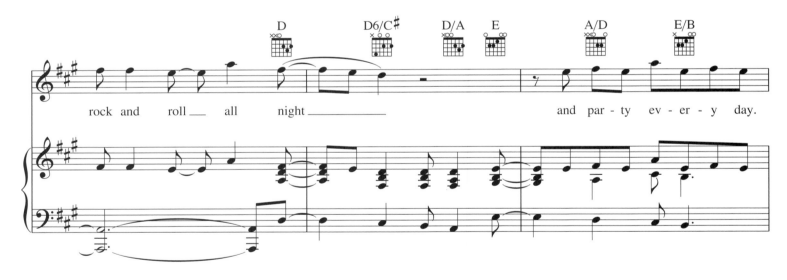

and par - ty ev - er - y day. I wan - na rock and roll _ all night _

and par - ty ev - er - y day.

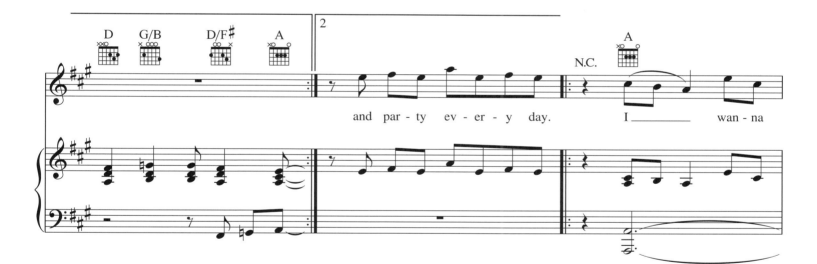

and par - ty ev - er - y day. I _____ wan - na

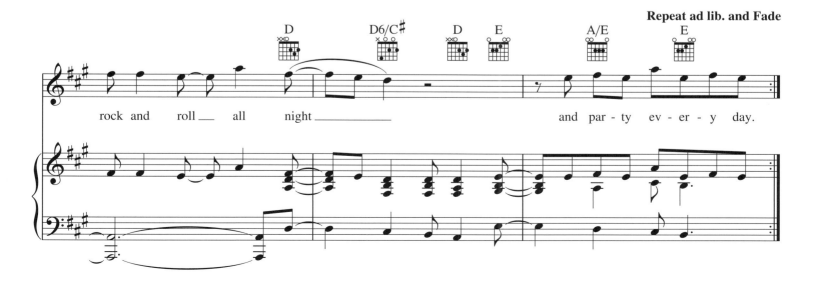

Repeat ad lib. and Fade

rock and roll _ all night _____ and par - ty ev - er - y day.

SHOUT

Words and Music by O'KELLY ISLEY,
RONALD ISLEY and RUDOLPH ISLEY

say you will. _____ Don't for - get to

say yeah, yeah, ___ yeah, yeah, ___ yeah. Say _____

____ you will. ___ Say it right now, ba - by. Say _____

____ you will. ___ Come on, _____ come on. _____ Say _____

you will ___ hey, ___ hey, ___ hey. Say ___

___ you will. ___ Come on ___ now. _____ (Say) Say that you
(Say) Say that you

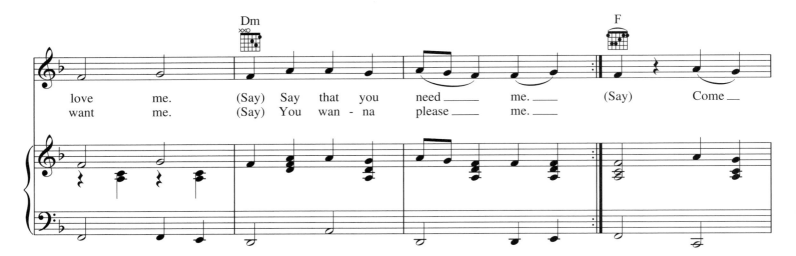

love me. (Say) Say that you need ___ me. ___ (Say) Come ___
want me. (Say) You wan - na please ___ me. ___

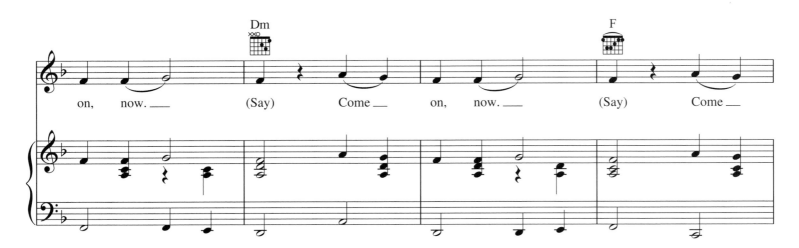

on, now. ___ (Say) Come ___ on, now. ___ (Say) Come ___

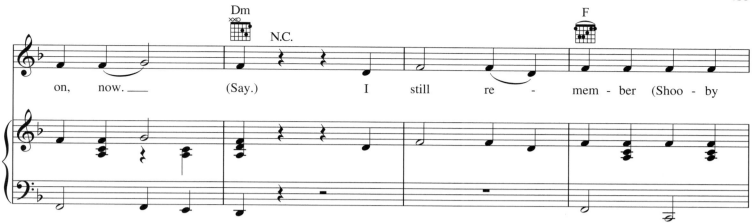

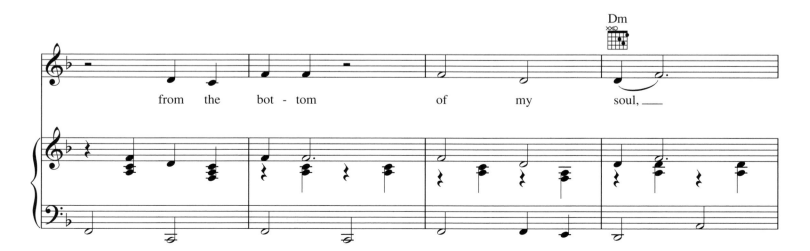

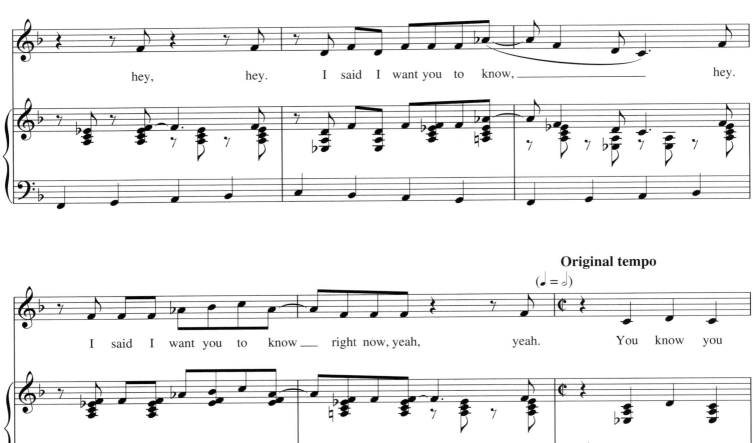

hey,   hey.   I said I want you to know, _____ hey.

I said I want you to know __ right now, yeah,   yeah.   You know you

Original tempo
($\quad = \quad$)

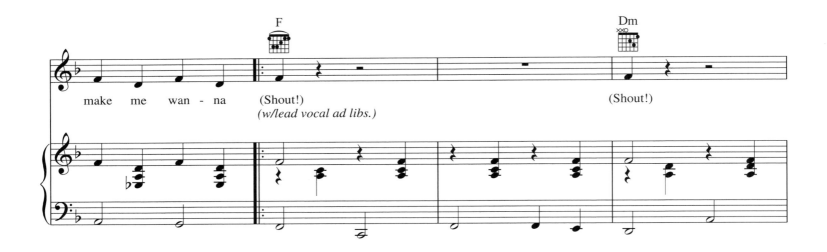

F

make me wan-na   (Shout!)   (Shout!)
(w/lead vocal ad libs.)

Dm

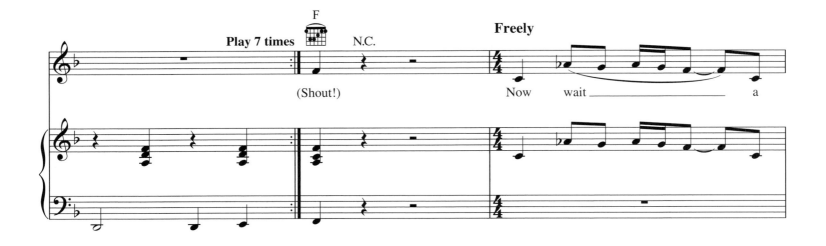

F
Play 7 times   N.C.   **Freely**

(Shout!)   Now wait _____ a

min - ute.   I feel   all _____

right. _____ (Yeah, yeah, yeah, yeah, yeah,   yeah.) Now that I've got my wom-an, I   feel   all _____

_____   right. _ (Yeah, yeah, yeah, yeah, yeah.) Ev-'ry time I think a - bout you,

Original tempo

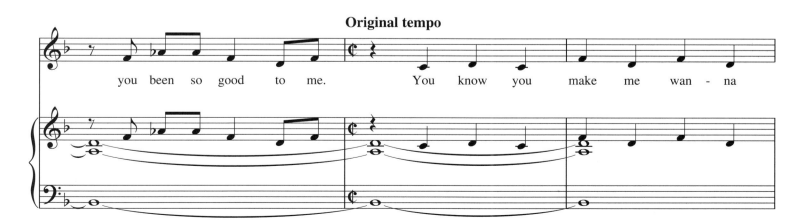

you been so good   to me.   You   know   you   make   me   wan - na

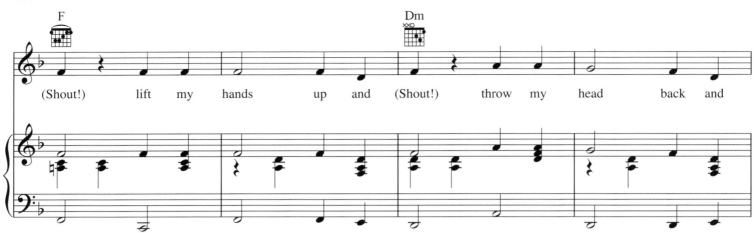

(Shout!) lift my hands up and (Shout!) throw my head back and

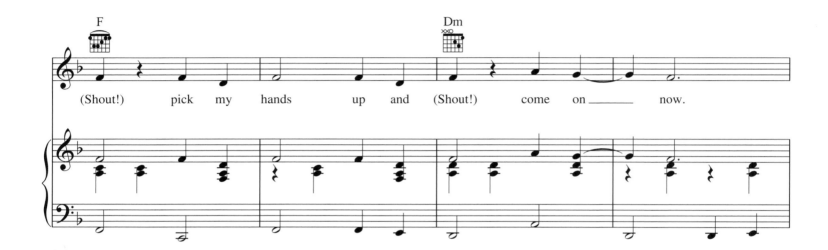

(Shout!) pick my hands up and (Shout!) come on _____ now.

(Shout!) Take it eas - y. (Shout!) Take it eas - y.

(Shout!) Take it eas - y. (Shout!) A lit - tle bit

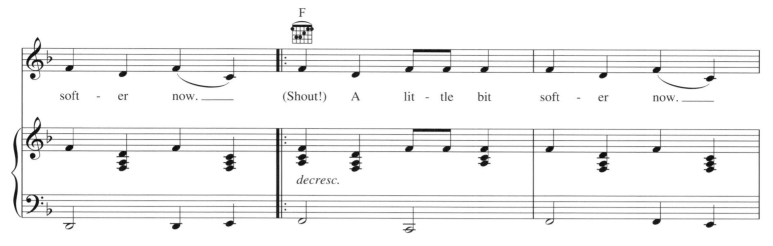

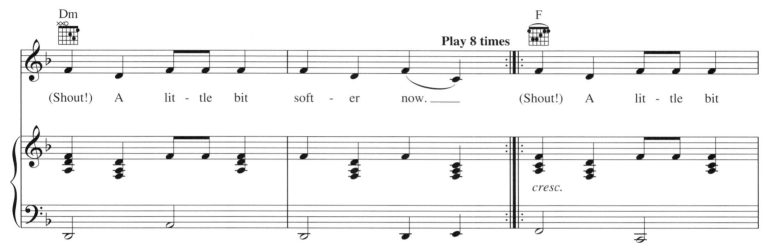

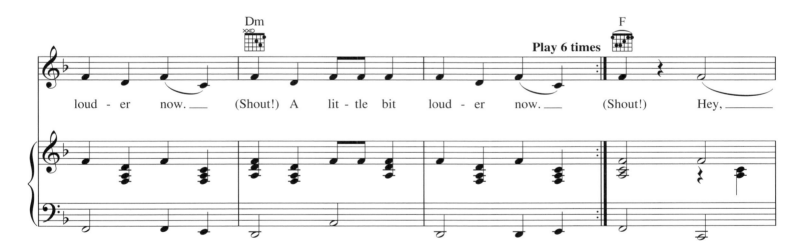

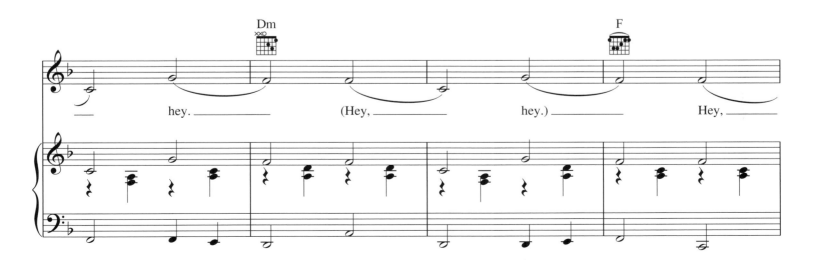

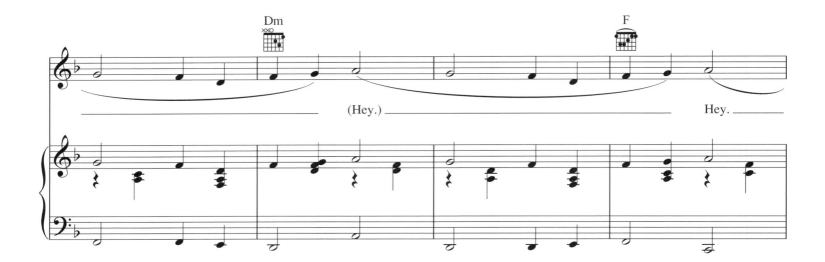

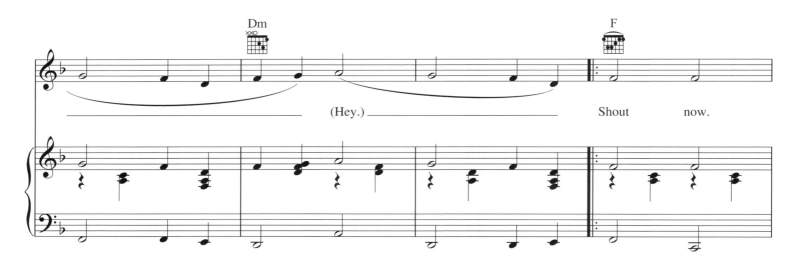

SOUL MAN

Words and Music by ISAAC HAYES
and DAVID PORTER

Com-in' to you on a
what I got on the
brought up on a

dust-y road, good lov-in' I got a truck-load. And
hard way, and I'll make it bet-ter each and ev-'ry day.
side street. I learned how to love be-fore I could eat. I was

grab your rope __ and I'll pull you in, __ give you hope __ and

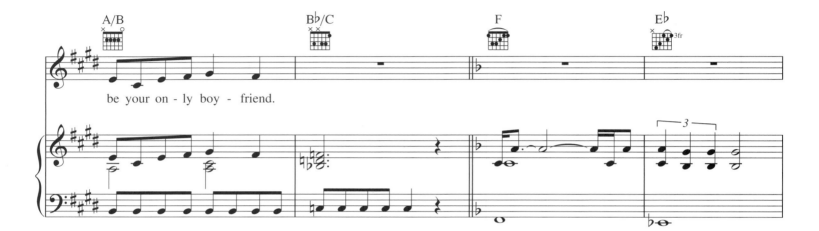

be your on - ly boy - friend.

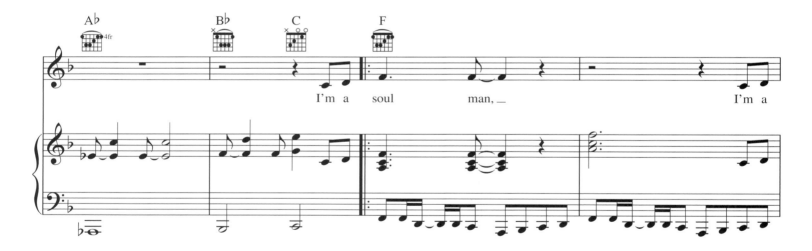

I'm a soul man, __ I'm a

soul man. __ I'm a

SUPER FREAK

Words and Music by RICK JAMES
and ALONZO MILLER

Moderately fast

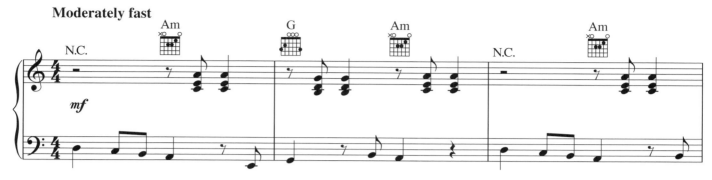

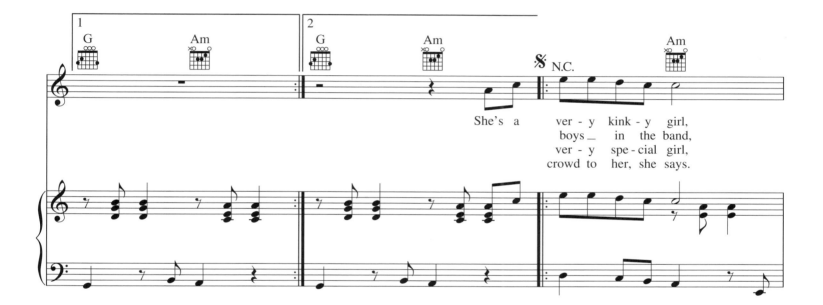

She's a ver-y kink-y girl,
boys__ in the band,
ver-y spe-cial girl,
crowd to her, she says.

the kind you don't take home to Moth-er. She will
she says that I'm her all-time fa-v'rite. When I
from her head down to her toe-nails. And she'll
"Room sev-en four-teen; I'll be wait-ing." When I

never let your spir - its down, _____ once you get her off ___ the street.
make my move to her room, it's the right time; she's nev-er hard _ to please.
wait for me at back-stage with her girl - friends in a lim - ou- sine.
get there she's got in - cense, wine and can - dles; it's such a freak - y scene.

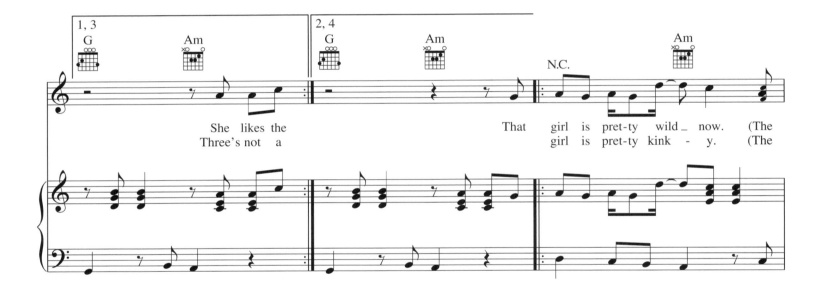

She likes the That girl is pret-ty wild _ now. (The
Three's not a girl is pret-ty kink - y. (The

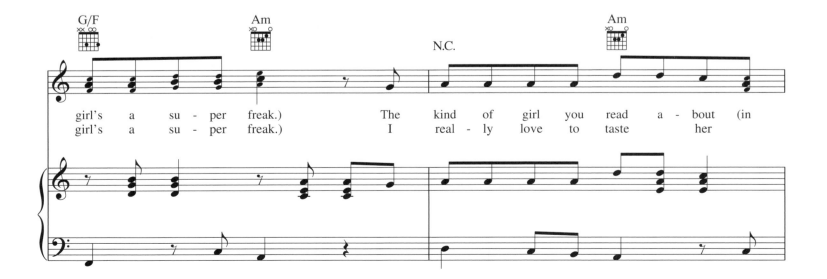

girl's a su - per freak.) The kind of girl you read a - bout (in
girl's a su - per freak.) I real - ly love to taste her

new wave mag - a- zines.) That (ev - 'ry time we meet.) She's all right, ___

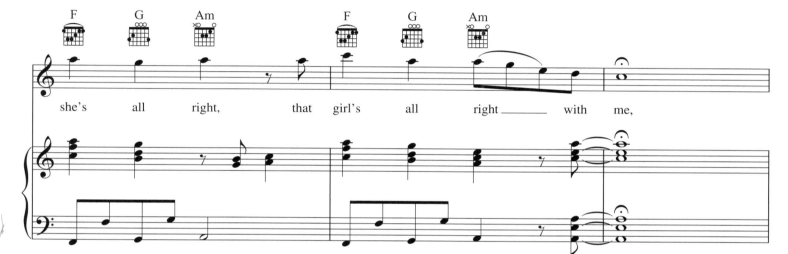

she's all right, that girl's all right _____ with me,

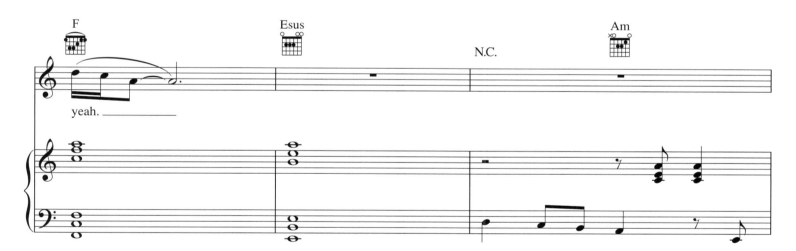

yeah. _____

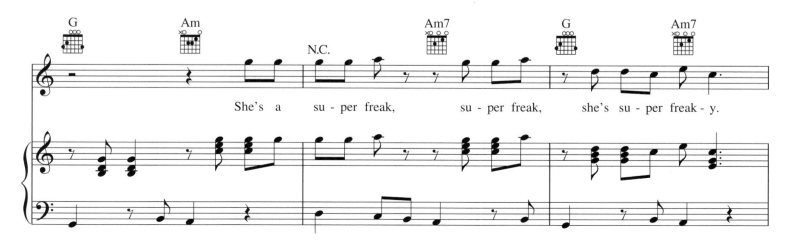

She's a su - per freak, su - per freak, she's su - per freak - y.

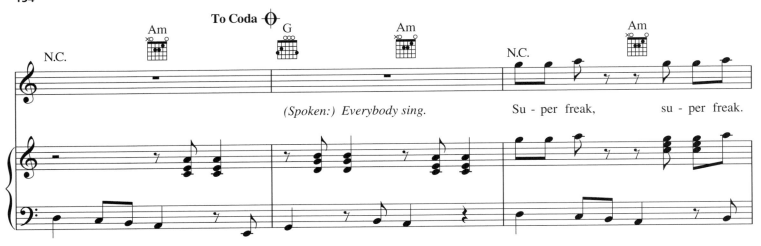

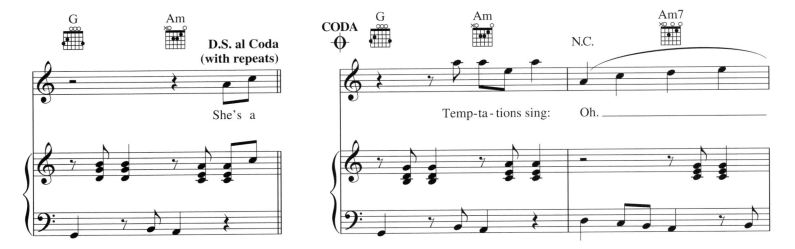

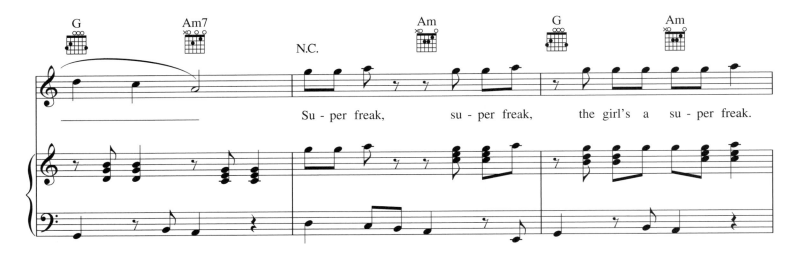

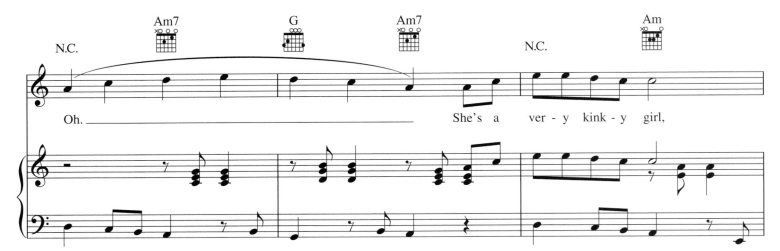

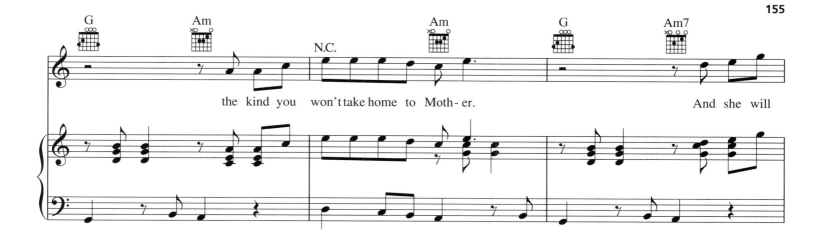

the kind you won't take home to Moth-er.   And she will

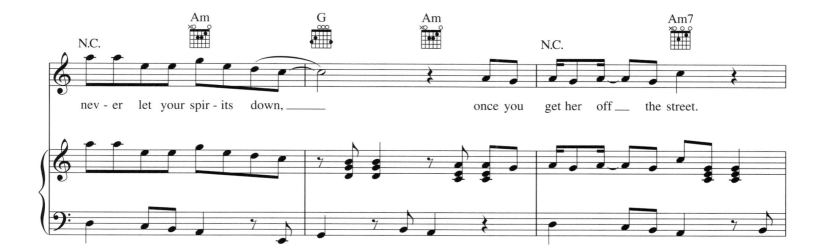

nev-er let your spir-its down, _____   once you get her off __ the street.

Sax solo ad lib.

Repeat and Fade   **Optional Ending**

THE TWIST

Words and Music by
HANK BALLARD

TWIST AND SHOUT

Words and Music by BERT RUSSELL
and PHIL MEDLEY

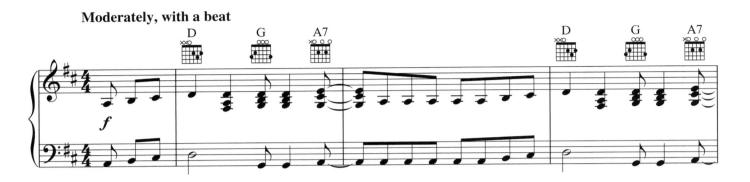

Well, shake it up ba - by, __ now,
- by, __ now, } (Shake it up ba - by) Twist and
- by, __ now,

shout. ____ (Twist and shout) ____ Come on, come on, __ come on, ___ come on,

ba - by, _____ now, Come on and work it on out. _____
(Come on, ba - by) (Work it on out)

(1.) Well, work it on out, _____ (Work it on out) _____
(2., 3.) You know you twist, lit - tle girl, _____ (Twist, lit - tle girl) _____

_____ You know you look so good. _____ (Look so good) _____ You know you got me
_____ You know you twist so fine. _____ (Twist so fine) _____ Come on and twist a lit - tle

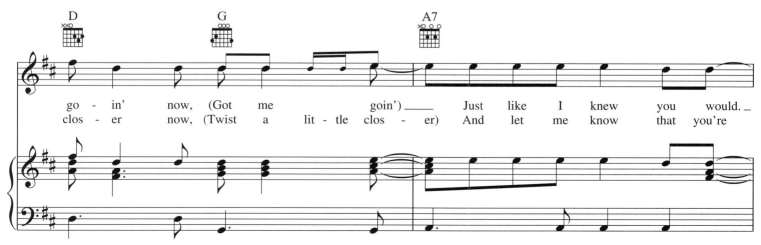

go - in' now, (Got me goin') _____ Just like I knew you would. _
clos - er now, (Twist a lit - tle clos - er) And let me know that you're

(Like I knew you would) ___
mine. (Let me know you're mine)   Well, shake it up ba-

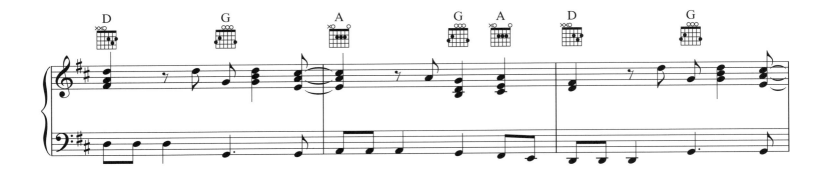

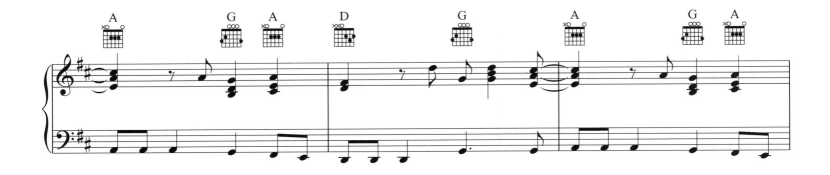

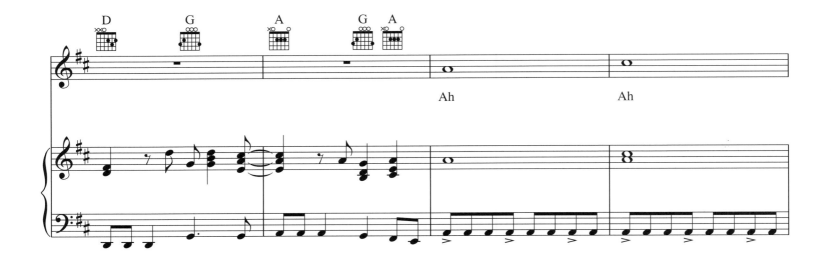

Ah   Ah

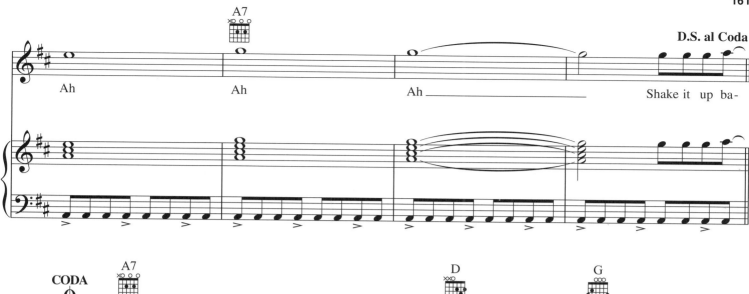

WALKING ON SUNSHINE

Words and Music by
KIMBERLEY REW

Bright Rock

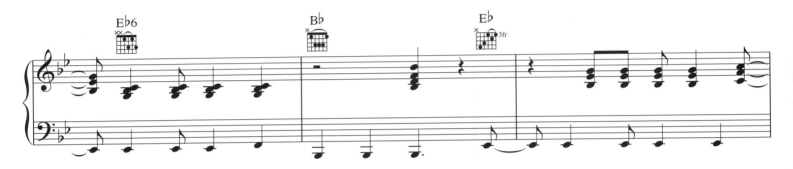

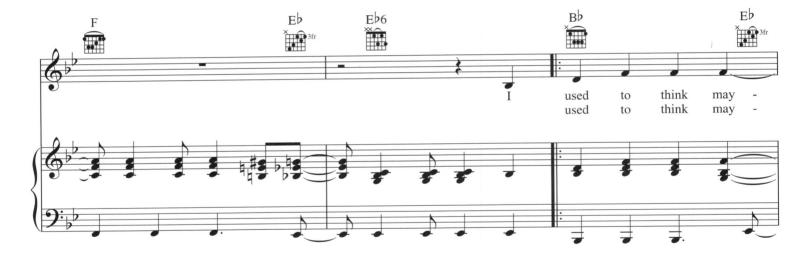

I used to think may -
used to think may -

- be you loved _____ me, now, ba - by, I'm _____ sure.
- be you loved _____ me, now I know that it's true. _____

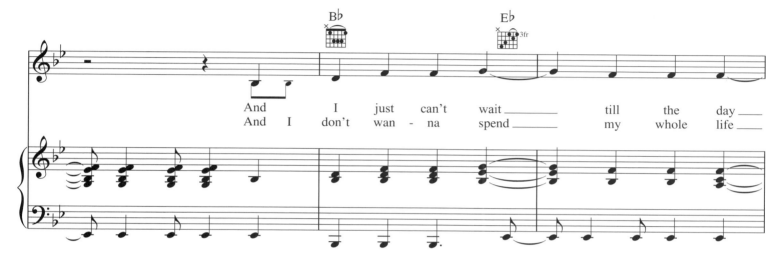

And   I   just   can't   wait _____   till   the   day _____

And   I   don't   wan - na   spend _____   my   whole   life _____

_____   when   you   knock _____   on   my   door. _____

_____   just   a - wait -   ing   for   you. _____

Now   ev - 'ry   time   I   go   for   the   mail -

Now   I   don't   want   you   back _____   for   the   week -

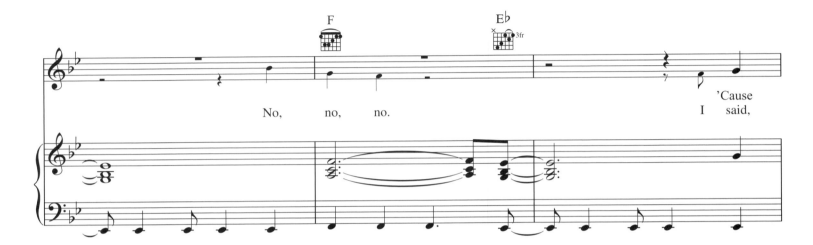

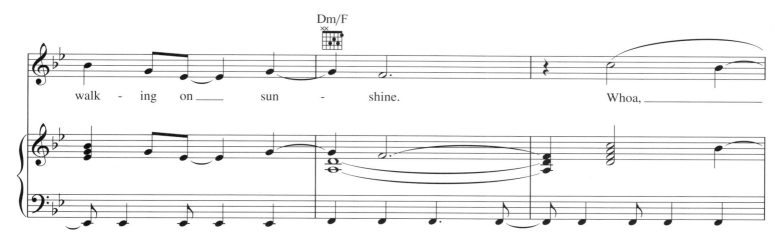

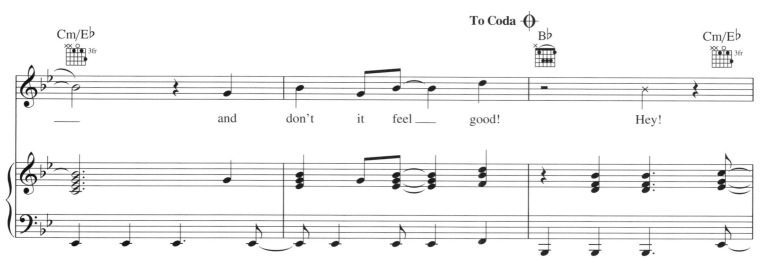

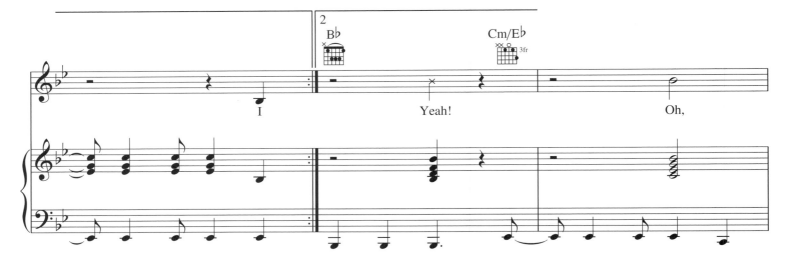

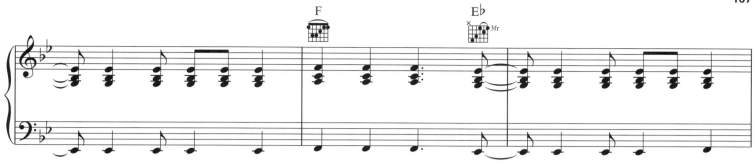

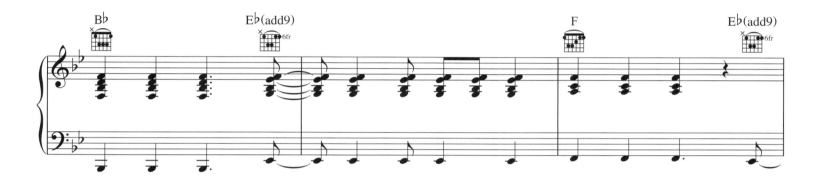

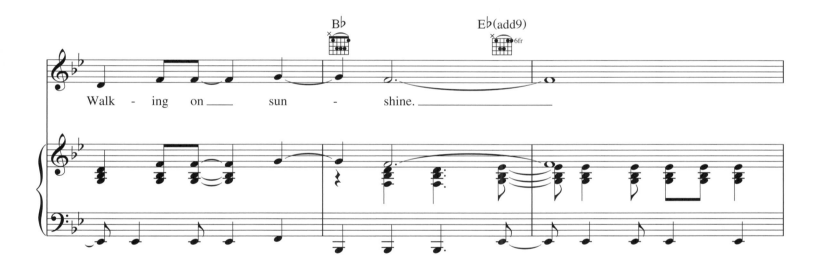

Walk - ing on ___ sun - shine. ___

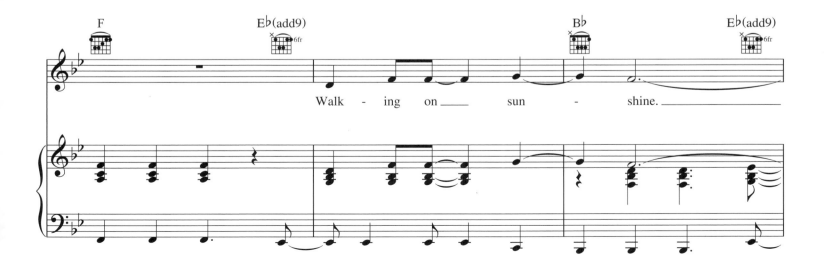

Walk - ing on ___ sun - shine. ___

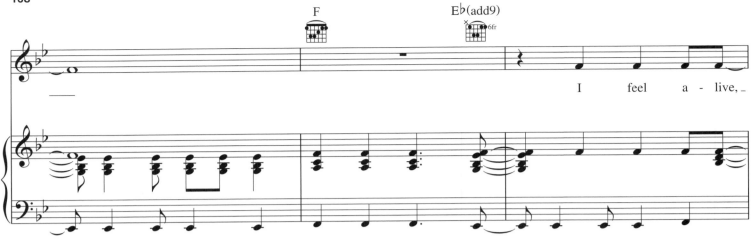

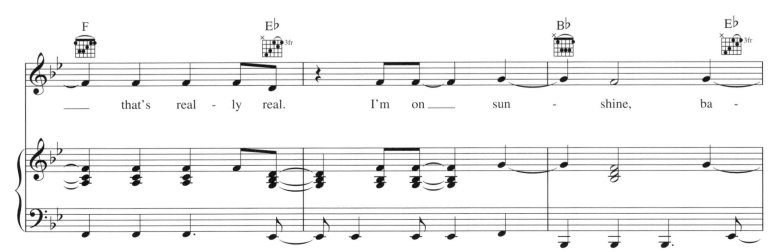

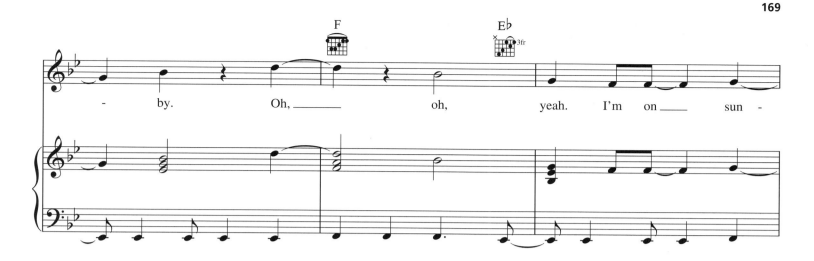

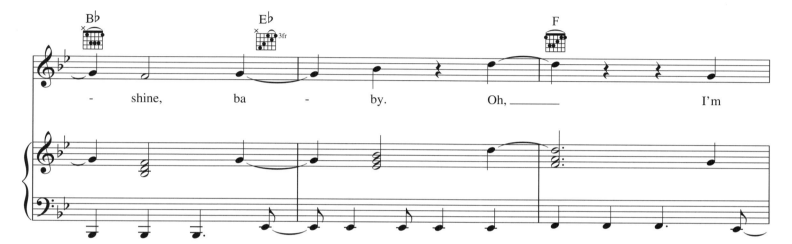

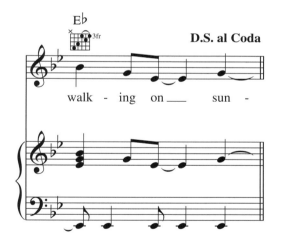

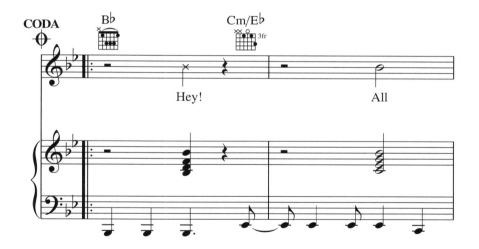

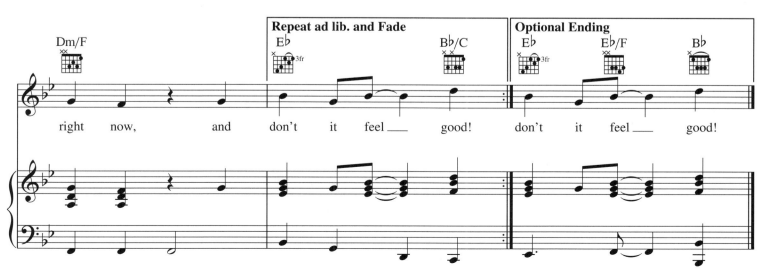

WE'RE NOT GONNA TAKE IT

Words and Music by
DANIEL DEE SNIDER

right to choose _ and there ain't no way we'll lose _ it. _
con - de-scend - ing, your gall is nev - er - end - ing. _

This is our life; _ this is _ our song. _
We don't want noth - in', not a thing _ from you. _

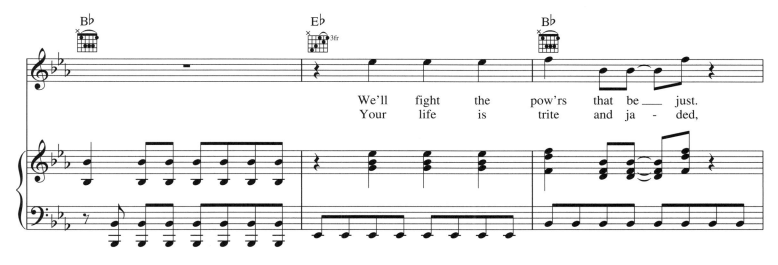

We'll fight the pow'rs that be _ just.
Your life is trite and ja - ded,

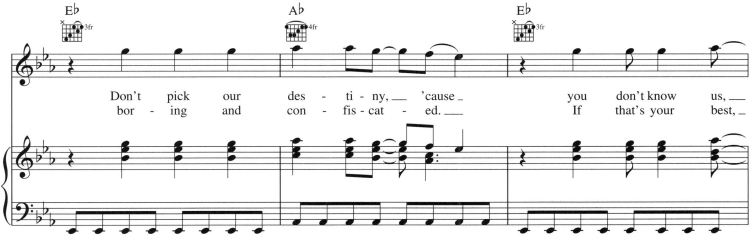

Don't pick our des - ti - ny, _ 'cause _ you don't know us, _
bor - ing and con - fis - cat - ed. _ If that's your best, _

We're right, yeah! We're free, yeah! We'll fight, yeah! You'll

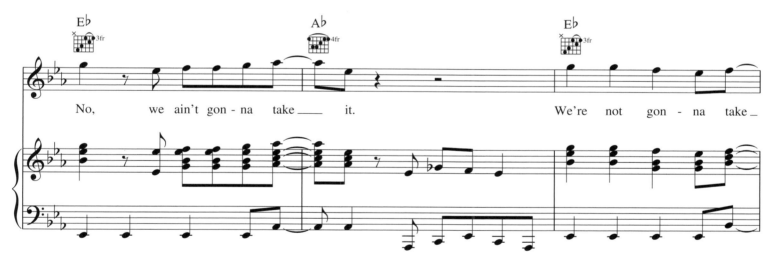

see. _____ Oh. _____ We're not gon - na take ___ it.

No, we ain't gon - na take ___ it. We're not gon - na take ___

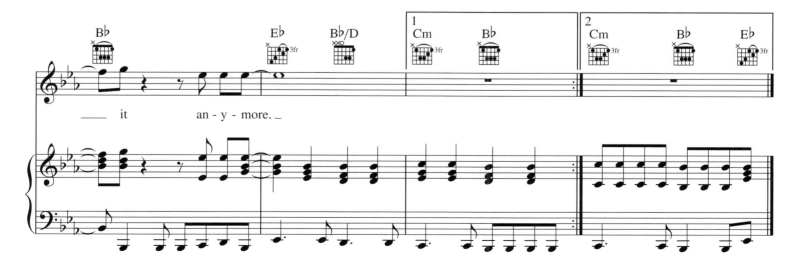

___ it an - y - more. ___

WHAT I LIKE ABOUT YOU

Words and Music by MICHAEL SKILL,
WALLY PALAMARCHUK and JAMES MARINOS

Bright Rock

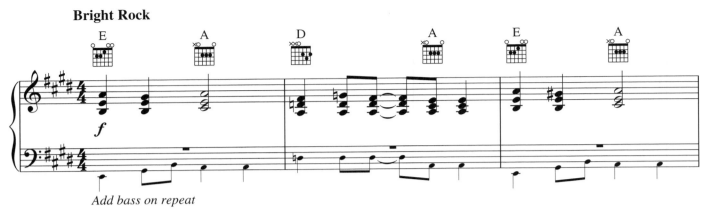

Add bass on repeat

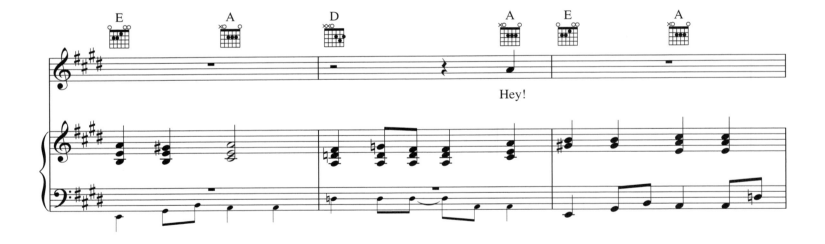

Hey!

unh - huh. ____   Hey!

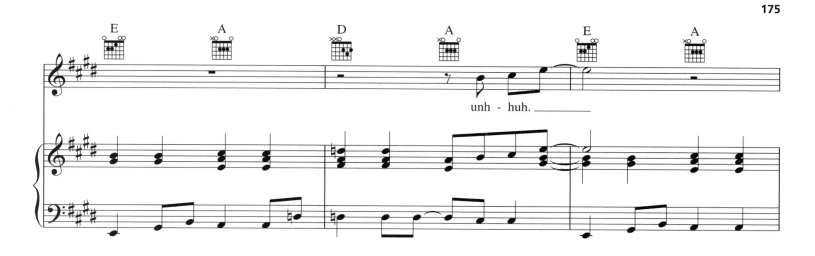

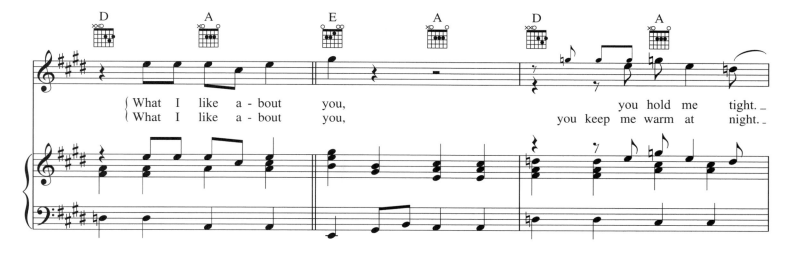

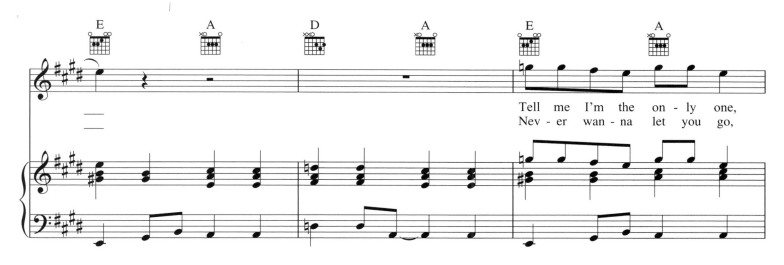

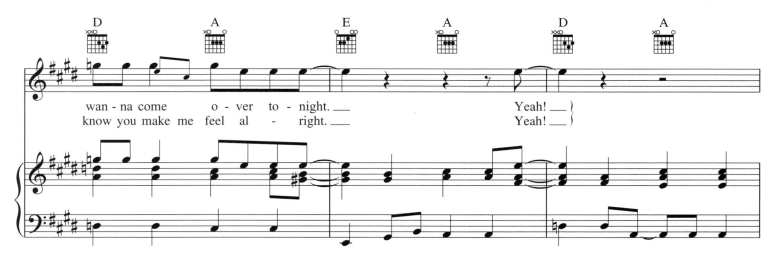

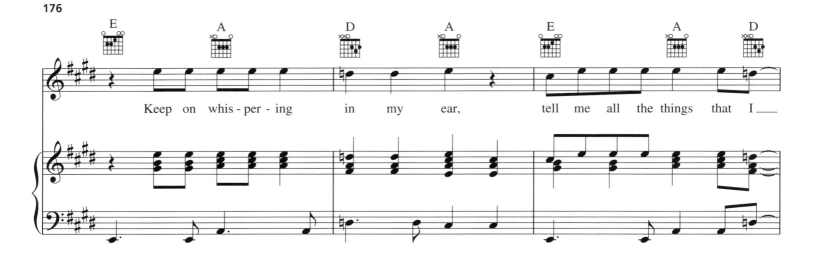

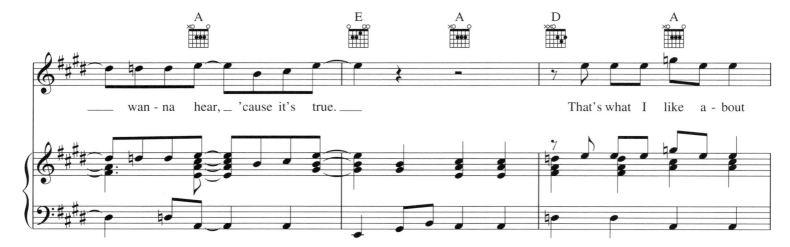

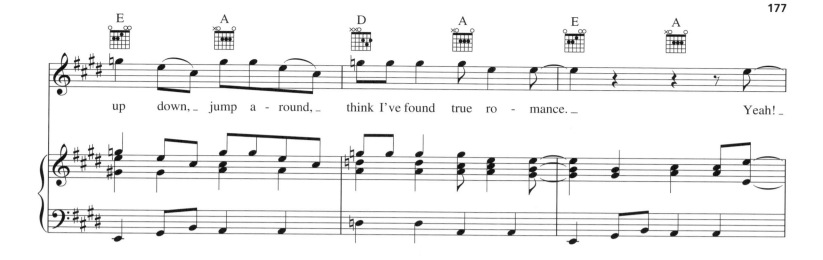

up down,_ jump a - round,_ think I've found true ro - mance._ Yeah!_

Keep on whis - per - ing in my ear,

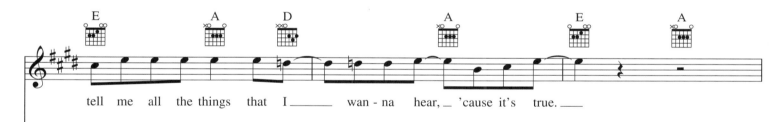

tell me all the things that I_____ wan - na hear,_ 'cause it's true.___

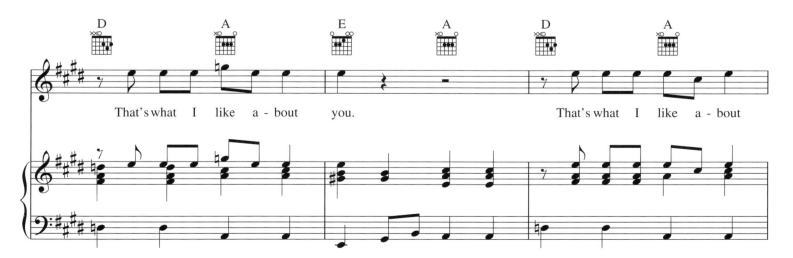

That's what I like a - bout you. That's what I like a - bout

178

you.   That's what I like a-bout   you.

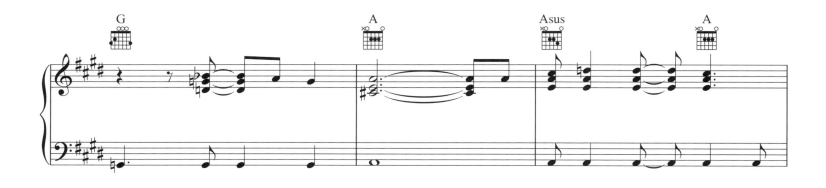

(Scream)

D.C. al Coda

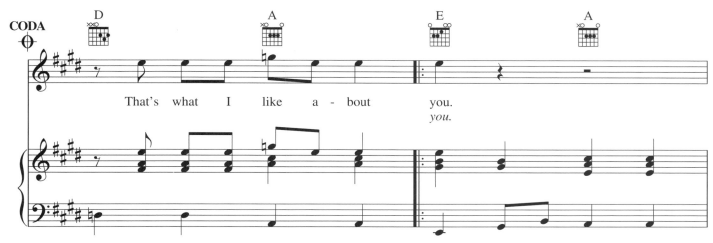

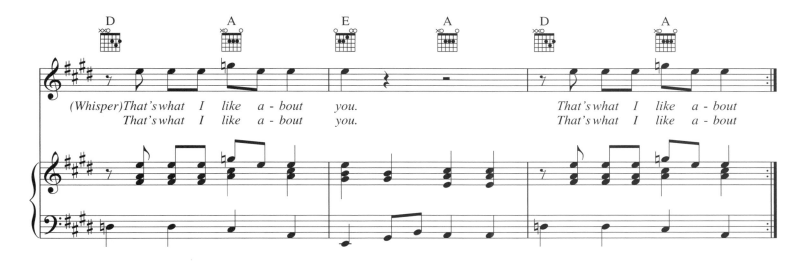

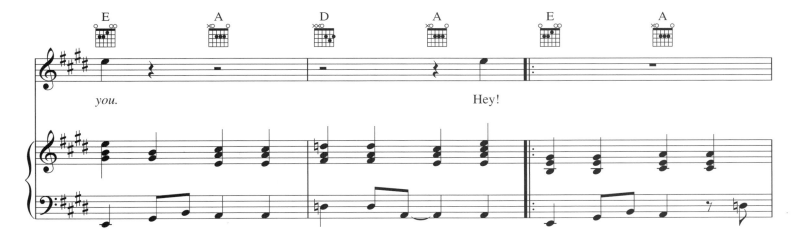

YELLOW SUBMARINE

Words and Music by JOHN LENNON
and PAUL McCARTNEY

March tempo

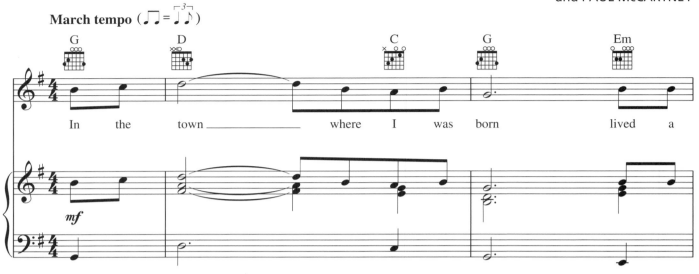

In the town _____ where I was born lived a

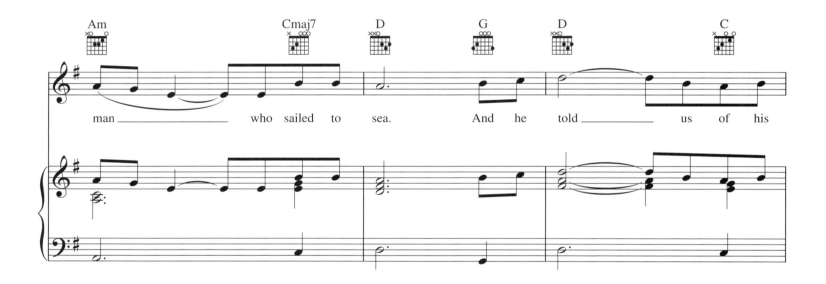

man _____ who sailed to sea. And he told _____ us of his

life in the land _____ of sub - ma - rines. So we

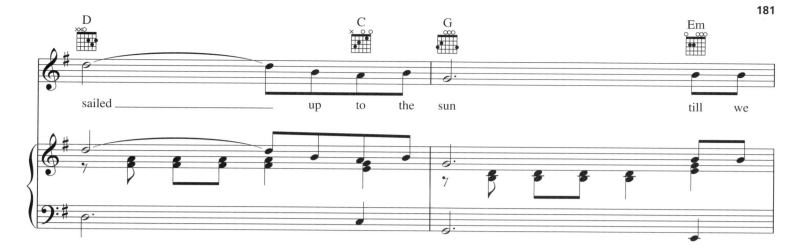

sailed _____ up to the sun _____ till we

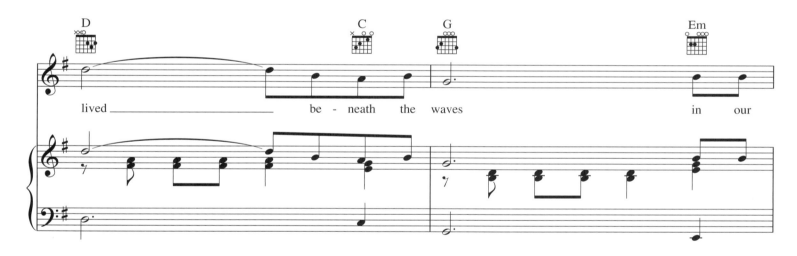

found _____ the sea of green. And we

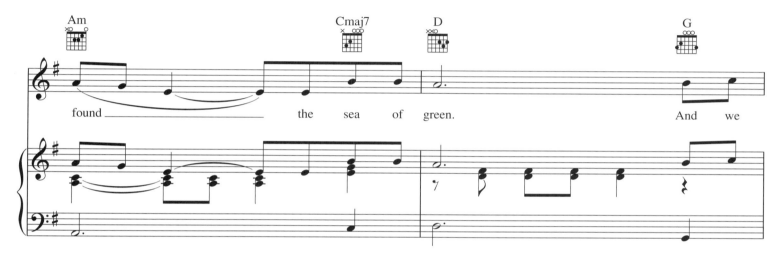

lived _____ be-neath the waves in our

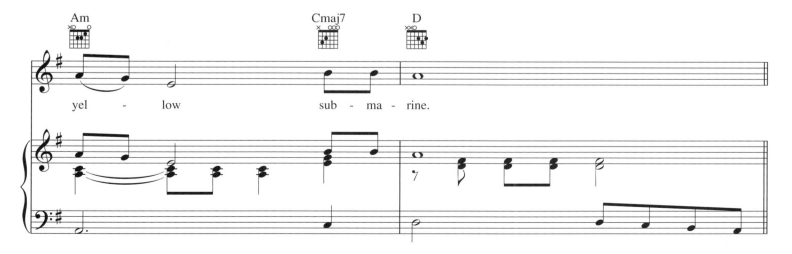

yel - low sub - ma - rine.

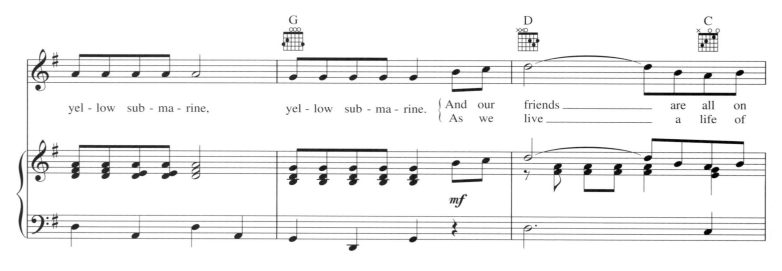

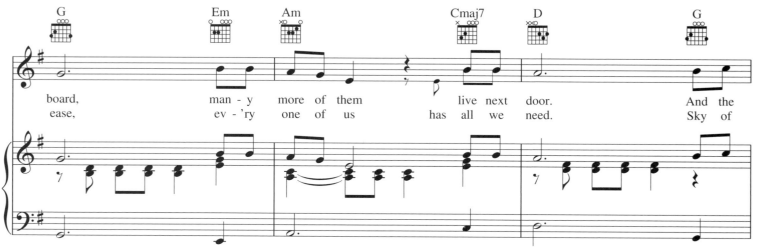

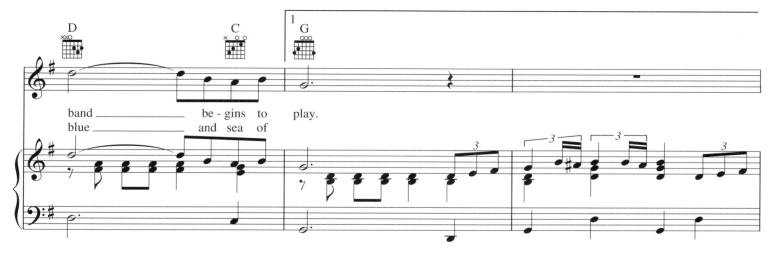

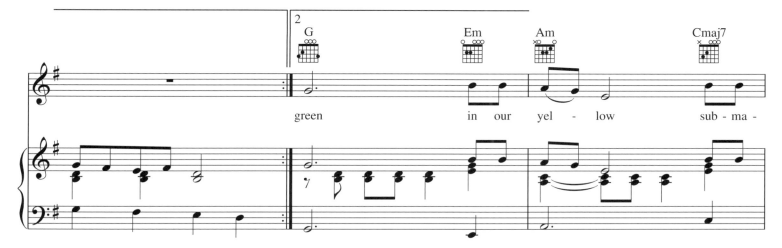

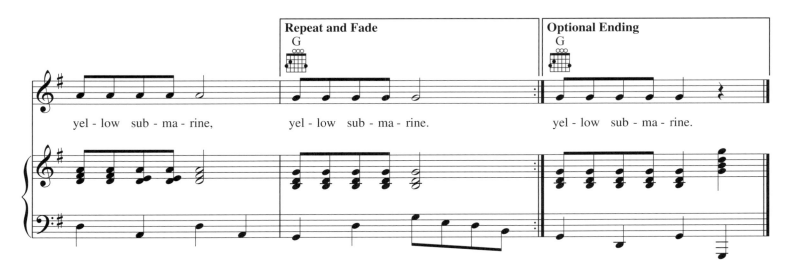

Y.M.C.A.

Words and Music by JACQUES MORALI,
HENRI BELOLO and VICTOR WILLIS

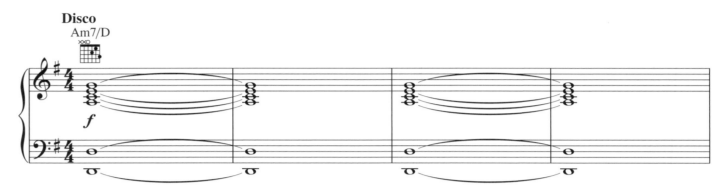

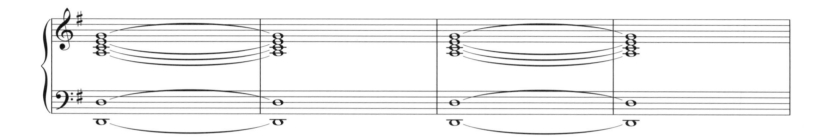

1. Young man,   there's no
2., 3. (See additional lyrics)

need to feel down. ___ I said, young man, pick your -

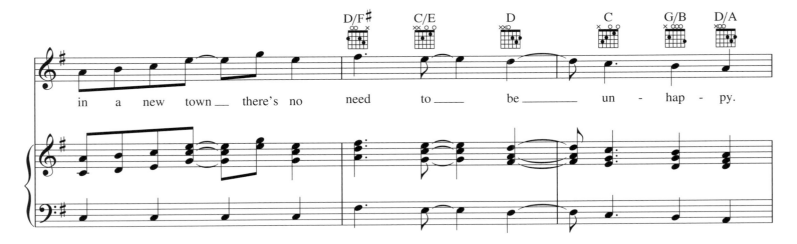

self off the ground. ___ I said, young man, 'cause you're

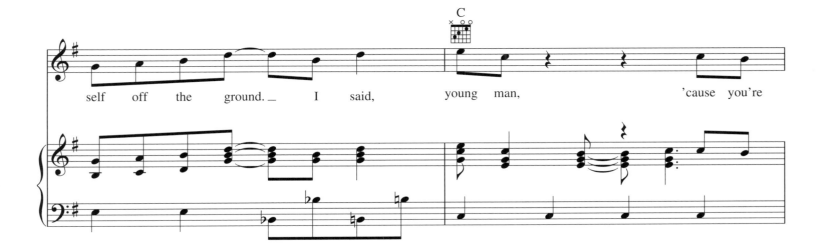

in a new town ___ there's no need to ___ be ___ un - hap - py.

Young man, there's a place you can go, ___ I said,

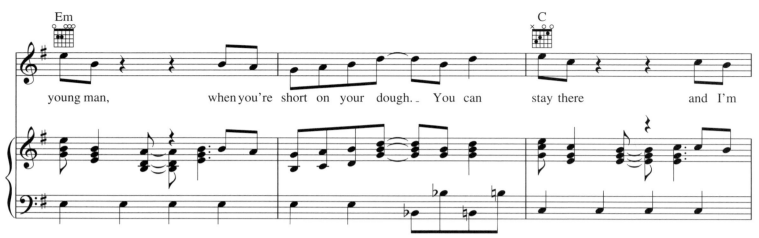

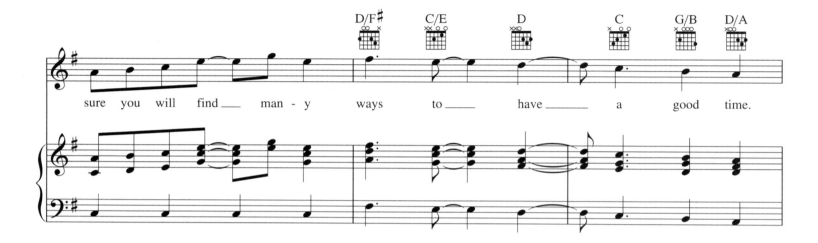

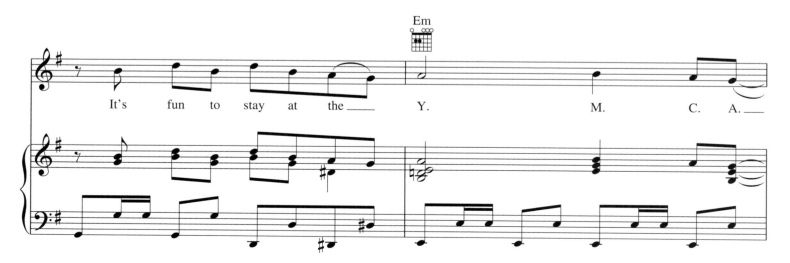

They have ev - er - y - thing _ for young

men to en - joy. _ You can hang out with all _ the boys. _

_ It's fun to stay at the Y. M. C. A.

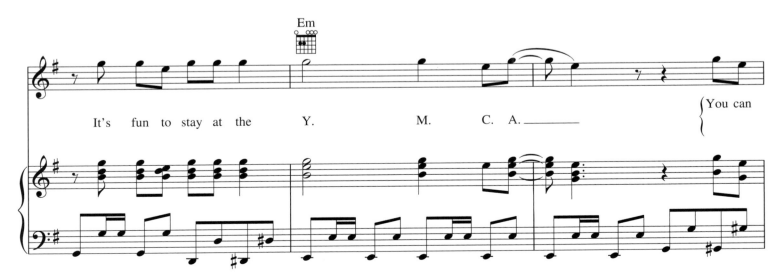

It's fun to stay at the Y. M. C. A. _ You can

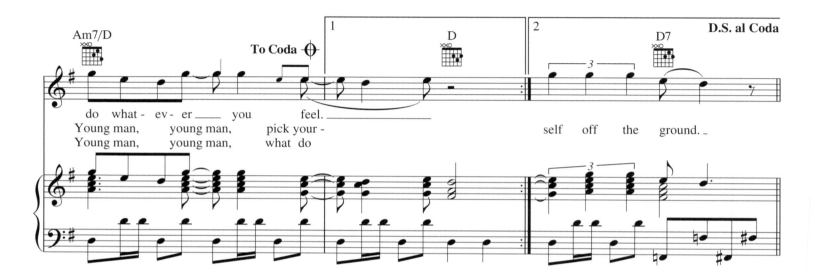

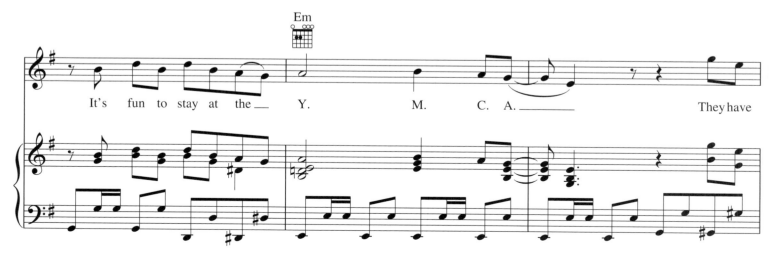

ev - er - y - thing ___ for young men to en - joy. ___ You can

Repeat ad lib. and Fade

hang out with all ___ the boys. ___ It's fun to stay at the

Additional Lyrics

2. Young man, are you listening to me?
   I said, young man what do you want to be?
   I said, young man you can make real your dreams
   But you've got to know this one thing.

   No man does it all by himself.
   I said young man put your pride on the shelf.
   And just go there to the Y.M.C.A.
   I'm sure they can help you today.
   Chorus

3. Young man, I was once in your shoes
   I said, I was down and out and with the blues.
   I felt no man cared if I were alive.
   I felt the whole world was so jive.

   That's when someone come up to me
   And said, "Young man, take a walk up the street.
   It's a place there called the Y.M.C.A.
   They can start you back on your way."
   Chorus

TEQUILA

By CHUCK RIO

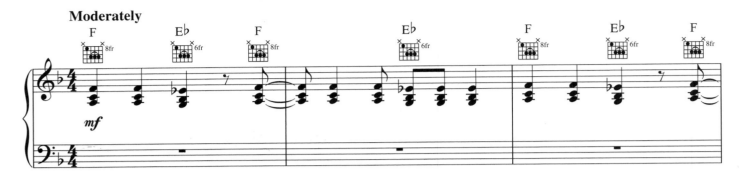

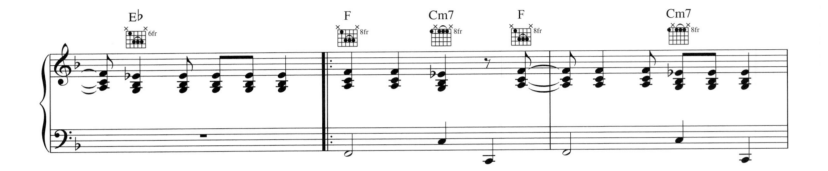

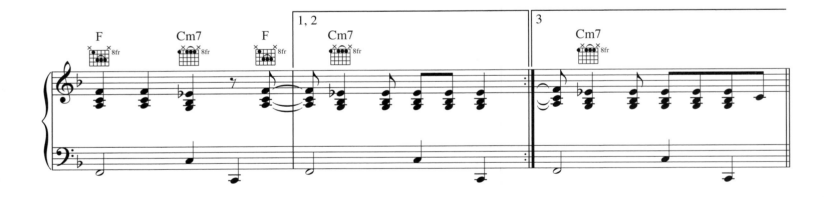

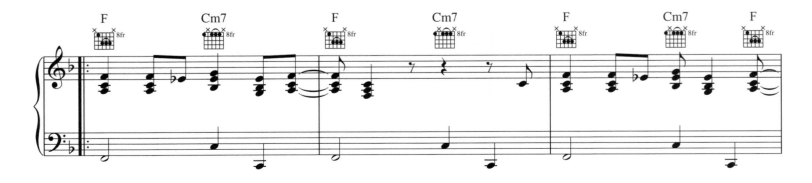